65 PROMISES FROM GOD

for your

CHILD

MIKE SHREVE

CHARISMA
HOUSE

Parenting can be one of the greatest challenges in life, but there is comfort in resting on the strength of our Lord. It is easy to feel lost, inadequate, or uncertain as a parent, but these feelings are all a common prerequisite to the greatness you will achieve once you overcome them. Mike Shreve has written a comprehensive and uplifting prayer devotional of the blessings that God has on your life. For any parent who needs a reminder of the great future that God has designed for your family, I would highly recommend this book.

—MATTHEW BARNETT
PASTOR AND COFOUNDER, LOS ANGELES DREAM
CENTER

Thank you, Mike, Elizabeth, Destiny, and Seth, for having a part in this amazing book of miracles and realizing the truth and power of God's Word. Our family has been richly blessed by this book as our adult children are weaving their way through child rearing. Thank you, Shreve family!

—BOB AND JANE D'ANDREA
FOUNDER AND CEO, CHRISTIAN TELEVISION
NETWORK

Our greatest investment and contribution to the future of our planet is the quality of the children we parent. Children are not only God's heritage but also our divine stewardship responsibility as we are charged with producing righteous seed to impact the next generation. This book is a major contribution to our efforts in cultivating children through effective prayer and spiritual development. I highly recommend this work to all who love children and their destiny.

—MYLES MUNROE
PRESIDENT AND SENIOR PASTOR, BAHAMAS FAITH
MINISTRIES INTERNATIONAL

On the day I picked up this important book, I had just been counseling with a father who was being faced with the choice of pursuing hard after money and business, or pursuing hard after the call of God on his family and home. As a pastor I know firsthand that the enemy is out to annihilate the family unit and take our children as spoil. Mike Shreve and I share a similar call "to turn the hearts of the fathers to the children" (Luke 1:17), and his book is an excellent daily handbook for parents who are serious about following God's directive to lead their children in a godly way. My godly heritage is rich, and I am in ministry today because of a Holy Ghost–filled and directed mom and dad who made sure I was trained in the way I should go. Thank you, Mike, for championing this cause! You have God's own heart.

—DONNA SCHAMBACH
PRESIDENT, SCHAMBACH MINISTRIES

I really like this book! Why? Because it encourages me to see my role as a parent through the eyes and heart of God. He loves my children even more than I do—and He gives me His promises that have substance and provide a firm foundation for me to stand on as a parent. Mike has been a frequent guest on *It's a New Day*, and he's always a blessing. The series we did about God's promises for our children was a home run! These are promises that as a parent you wish God had given you, and then you discover He *has*!

—WILLARD THIESSEN
FOUNDER, TRINITY TELEVISION, WINNIPEG, CANADA

Cover design by Justin Evans
Design Director: Bill Johnson

Visit the author's website at www.shreveministries.org.

Library of Congress Cataloging-in-Publication Data:
Shreve, Mike.
  65 supernatural promises for your child / Mike Shreve. -- 1st ed.
    p. cm.
  Includes bibliographical references.
  ISBN 978-1-61638-960-4 (trade paper) -- ISBN 978-1-61638-961-1 (e-book)
 1. God--Promises--Biblical teaching. 2. Parents--Prayers and
devotions. 3. Children--Prayers and devotions. I. Title. II. Title:
Sixty-five supernatural promises for your child.
  BT180.P7S54 2013
  248.8'45--dc23

                                    2012041360

13 14 15 16 17 — 10 9 8 7 6 5 4
Printed in the United States of America

I dedicate this book to my children, Zion Seth and Destiny Hope. Your mom and I love you more than words can say. Being your parents actually awakened within our hearts the truths in this book. We pray and confess that every promise within these pages will be fulfilled in your lives.

_____

(Your Name)

dedicates this book to

_____

(Child's Name)

on

_____

(Date)

May the everlasting God watch over
these promises to fulfill them in your life
and the lives of all of your offspring!

CONTENTS

FOREWORD

IREMEMBER WAITING WITH anticipation as I stared down at that little white strip, hoping and praying that this time it would be positive and not negative like all the other ones before it. Then it happened. The pregnancy test registered positive, and immediately my heart was filled with both excitement and fear. As the days progressed, I must admit that fear took the lead. I was filled with questions: *Can I handle the responsibility? Can I do this right? Can I be a good mother?*

That was about twenty-one years ago, and I wish I could say I know everything about parenting, but nothing could be further from the truth. I've read a lot of books, ordered dozens of magazines, and even attended parenting classes. All those tools have been a great blessing to me, but they are not enough on their own. I've had days of great joy and days of great pain as a parent. The resources I found helped me only to a limited degree during the more difficult times. But there is one parenting tool that has always stood out from the rest: the Word of God. This Book of all books always has been my sustaining force.

My first pregnancy was extremely taxing on my body. I was in my "Wonder Woman" phase. I thought I could do it all. I thought I could travel in ministry with Mike just like before. We were preaching constantly, and I was running an office and managing a household. Needless to say, I was exhausted.

Eventually my Wonder Woman phase turned into just a "wonder" phase. I wondered, "How on earth will I do all of this?" While in prayer, I sensed the Holy Spirit speak to me from Psalm 27:13: "I would have fainted, unless I had believed that I would see the goodness of the LORD in the land of the living" (KJV21). Praise God! It was God's goodness that caused me not to faint.

I gave birth to a wonderful son. Seth has been goodness to me. He is intelligent and witty. His future is so bright in God. Yes, the Word of the Lord is my sustaining force.

With Destiny, the situation was totally different. It wasn't *my* body in jeopardy; it was hers. From the beginning we faced a constant stream of negative doctors' reports. There was always something new. This was wrong; that was wrong. Then we received the most terrible reports of all. Our baby girl had spina bifida and cretinism (a hole in her spine and, most likely, severe retardation). The doctor and his assistant claimed that she would never be normal, that she probably would never walk or speak. That physician, knowing we were Christian leaders, even had the audacity to lean across his desk and suggest an "alternative" to carrying the baby to term.

As we left his office (by the way, we never returned to him), I heard the voice of the Lord say, "*Your daughter will dance on the streets of Jerusalem*" (totally the opposite of what we had just been told). Then, as we sat in our car, I turned on the radio. Amazingly, the first thing that played was the song "I Hope You Dance." What a confirmation! My spirit leapt within me. God had clearly revealed that He was going to intervene.

I must admit, however, that even though I had received a powerful word from God, I still faced an overwhelming frontal assault of fears and doubts. Once again I turned to my sustaining force. After weeks of warring against a whirlwind of worry and dread, I was finally able to fix my focus on the thing that gives life—the Word of God. I began to quote Psalm 138:8 often: "The LORD will perfect that which concerns me."

I started laying hands on my belly, saying, "You are perfect, little girl. The Word of God says you are perfect. You concern me—therefore, according to God's Word, you are perfect." Praise God, when Destiny was born, the first words the doctor said were, "She's perfect." And she was. Not only that, but also from a young age she has expressed herself as a real lover of God, a worshipper, and a gifted dancer—just as God said. I just praise the Lord for His goodness!

It is the Word that brings forth the miraculous. Hold it close to your heart. Declare it! Believe it! My difficult first steps in the drama of parenthood taught me a valuable lesson that has remained with me to this day. If we can successfully speak goodness and perfection over our children in natural things, then we can speak goodness and perfection over them in spiritual things as well. This wonderful book will empower you to do that very thing.

—ELIZABETH SHREVE

PREFACE

MY WIFE AND I have been blessed with two healthy, bright, wonderful children. They are both miracles. Our son's birth was very traumatic and should have damaged him irreparably, and our daughter was given a very dark prognosis before she was born. But, praise God, the doctors didn't have the last word—God did. Against all odds in the natural, they survived. My wife and I firmly believe that our faith in God is the reason our children are alive and thriving today. We sought God consistently and trusted Him to fulfill His promises—and He did just that.

At the time of this writing, our son, Zion Seth, is twenty, and our daughter, Destiny Hope, is eleven. They're good kids. They do well in school. They love God. But my wife and I still face plenty of challenges as parents. Our fight of faith is not over, and we constantly find ourselves grasping for promises in God's Word that relate to our daily circumstances. We have discovered that the Bible is our "anchor" (Heb. 6:19)—not only during the major storms of life but also in the minor problems and conflicts, those "gusty winds" that sweep in unexpectedly.

Getting acquainted with God's Word is, in a spiritual sense, like putting up storm windows and storm doors on our homes. God warned, "My people are destroyed for lack of knowledge" (Hosea 4:6). How often this proves to be true! If we as parents do not know what God has said concerning our children, we have no basis for our faith. Then when the wind starts blowing, we're vulnerable the glass shatters, the doors blow open, and life is filled with chaos.

You may feel you're at a point like that right now. You might even be tempted to give up on parenthood, give up on your children, and throw in the towel. Don't do it! Grab that towel. Dry your tears. Refocus. Get adamant. Reclaim your seed.

In Exodus 10 Pharaoh agreed to let the Israelite men leave Egypt to worship God in the wilderness, but he told Moses their sons and daughters would have to stay behind. Moses's response was quick and definite:

No way! They would not worship God without their children. In the same way you need to inform the prince of darkness, "You can't have my children! I'm not leaving them behind! As for me and my house, we will serve the Lord!"

Are you beginning to feel a surge of spiritual adrenaline just by thinking those kinds of determined thoughts? Is faith rising up within you? Don't just think those thoughts. Declare that God has the victory in your home.

In this book are sixty-five promises God has given concerning the offspring of the righteous. I encourage you to devour every word. Let it become a part of you. Learn God's promises; then start fighting the good fight of faith for your seed. You can do it! The victory is in sight.

A MIRACLE FOR YOUR FAMILY

*Miracle: An extraordinary event manifesting
divine intervention in human affairs.[1]*

GET READY TO get acquainted with a heart-warming, hope-filled sub-
ject in God's Word: the revelation of sixty-five promises God has
given concerning the offspring of His people. These are more than feel-
good scriptures to encourage you during tough times; these are powerful
truths that reveal God's heart for you as His child and your offspring.
God wants to work a miracle in your family as you declare His Word.

But before we explore these promises, we need to lay a firm foundation. We must first understand God's view of parenthood and how
it differs from ours, as well as how we can effectively appropriate the
promises He has given us. So let's begin by examining parenthood from
God's perspective.

GOD'S VIEW OF PARENTHOOD

Amazingly the first sign of the blessing of God on both animals and
humankind was the impartation of procreative power—the ability to
bring forth image-bearing offspring. Immediately after creating the animals, "God blessed them, saying, 'Be fruitful and multiply'" (Gen. 1:22).
After creating Adam and Eve, God made a similar statement but with
significant additions:

> Then God blessed them, and God said to them, "Be fruitful
> and multiply; fill the earth and subdue it; have dominion
> over the fish of the sea, over the birds of the air, and over
> every living thing that moves upon the earth."
>
> —GENESIS 1:28, MKJV

In this passage God not only manifested His blessing upon the fore-parents of the human race by empowering them to have children, but He also revealed His intention to use those children to further His purposes in the world. God's aim is still the same. He is determined to fill the earth with righteous, God-loving children who will subdue the evil in the earth and take dominion over spiritual darkness in the name of the Lord.

Children born into stable homes to parents with strong marriages are far more capable of consistently fulfilling this divine desire. In Malachi 2:15 God commands faithfulness in marriage. Then He explains the reason behind the mandate. He is seeking a "godly seed" (KJV). Infidelity in a home can have a dangerous and damaging effect on children, ultimately pushing them toward similar ungodly patterns of living. God is seeking parents who will leave a godly legacy, not a trail of dysfunction. The Contemporary English Version of this verse says it well:

> Didn't God create you to become like one person with your wife? And why did he do this? It was so you would have children, and then lead them to become God's people. Don't ever be unfaithful to your wife.

As the *Spirit-Filled Life Bible* explains, "When God chose to create man in His own image, He created a marriage, a family. The community of the family is a reflection of the community in the Godhead [the Father, Son, and Holy Spirit]. Its identity, life, and power come from God" (Eph. 3:14–15).[2] So let me reiterate this important truth: God is seeking parents with strong value systems who will perpetuate His righteous purposes in the earth, parents who will "become God's people" and leave their children a legacy of godliness.

This is high on God's list of priorities, because our time on earth will come to an end. Whatever ground is gained for Christianity in one generation can be totally lost in the next if the former generation fails to impart passion for the things of God to their children. So parenthood is a great blessing—not only to us but to God as well—because through our children the hope of God's people taking dominion and advancing His kingdom in the earth can live on, growing with each generation.

Our View of Parenthood

As we read earlier, the ability to procreate is a blessing from God, but parenting can feel overwhelming at times. Recently I saw a somewhat harried-looking woman walking through a discount store with a flock of kids. Her T-shirt read, "Who are these children, and why are they calling me Mom?" Maybe you're in a similar agitated state of mind. But living in denial won't help. Come to grips with it—you are a parent.

How you view the role God has called you to will make all the difference. Do you look at parenting as a burden, little more than a series of responsibilities to fulfill? If so, it will feel like an unwanted weight. Let me tell you, parenting is so much more than a role you fulfill! Solomon, the wisdom writer, gives us a wonderful insight into parenthood. He wrote, "Children are an inheritance from the Lord. They are a reward from him" (Ps. 127:3, GW).

In other words, children are one of God's most wonderful gifts; the fruit of the womb is an incomparable and generous legacy from on high. When tough times come and your offspring are not as well behaved as you would like, you might be tempted to think being a parent isn't such a blessing. But winning the battles of life—and the challenges of parenting—starts with a choice. You must choose to view parenting as God views it, and you must choose to believe—enough to make confessions of faith instead of declarations of doubt—that your children are a reward.

Speaking negatively over your children is actually a way of cursing them. If you carelessly predict a dark future scenario for your children, your words "nudge" them (sometimes "shove" them) toward that end. Don't do it! Even if your kids are stubborn and disrespectful, don't reinforce the negative by making statements such as:

+ "My children stress me out."

+ "My children are so rebellious."

- "My children just don't respect me."

- "My children are walking in darkness."

- "My children are in the hands of the enemy."

- "My children will never make it in life."

- "My children are caught in the world's web."

- "I'll be glad when they're out of the nest!"

Parents who repeatedly say, or even think, these things tend to weave a very dark, threefold cord around their own hearts—a cord of doubt, despair, and anger. Rid yourself of these binding attitudes right now and weave the opposite. As Zig Ziglar said, "When you put faith, hope, and love together, you can raise positive kids in a negative world."[3] Start by being very positive yourself and by boldly confessing God's will for your children:

- "My children are an inheritance from God!"

- "My children are part of the fruit I bear in life!"

- "My children are a reward from God!"

- "My children are a blessing!"

- "My children will walk in the light!"

- "My children are in the hands of God!"

- "My children will fulfill their destiny!"

- "My children will be used by God to change this world."

- "My children and I are building a relationship with permanent value!"

Parents cannot make proclamations like these unless they really believe what Psalm 127:3 says. I am sure you can identify many "gifts" from God in your life: your possessions, your abilities, your calling, your intellect. These are all wonderful, but none of them carry your genetic code. Your children do. The longer you live, the more you will grow to appreciate this mystery.

Appropriating the Promises

It is not enough to simply know the promises of God. You must also activate them in your child's life. Psalm 127:3 says your children are a blessing from God and a reward from Him. This tells me that He is very interested in your family. He wants these promises to manifest in their lives.

The world seems to be getting darker with each passing generation. Like a creature with many tentacles, spiritual darkness is wrapping itself around the minds and hearts of our youth. Multiplied thousands are being strangled by drugs, alcohol, sexual perversion, gang violence, the occult, intellectualism, false religions, and other diabolical plots and plans of the enemy.

Thankfully, in the midst of all of this danger, there is a place of protection, a place where our children can be preserved from harm. This refuge is in the promises God has given concerning the children of those parents who are in a covenant relationship with Him. When we dedicate our children to God, we place them under His divine influence and care.

My wife, Elizabeth, and I pray these promises over our children often. We urge you to do the same. Go through these divine pledges one by one. Commit them to memory and prayerfully speak them over your children whenever you can. Declaring these promises in faith will release them to manifest in your children's lives. Remember, Scripture teaches, "Death and life are in the power of the tongue, and those who love it will eat its fruit" (Prov. 18:21). We can choose to speak life or death over our offspring.

You may want to use this book as a daily devotional, either by yourself or with your child. You could focus on a new promise each day or study one promise every week. However you choose to meditate on these promises, when you finish this book you should fully comprehend—and, prayerfully, apprehend—all of these divine pledges.

Author E. M. Bounds correctly noted that "God's promises are dependent and conditioned upon prayer to appropriate them and make them a conscious realization. The promises are wrought in us, appropriated by us, and held in the arms of faith by prayer....Prayer gives the promises their efficiency, directs and appropriates them, and utilizes them. Prayer puts the promises to practical and present uses."[4]

Each promise in this book has a key scripture followed by an explanation of that promise that will help you put it into action in your life. Sometimes the same verse will contain several related promises. If so, that verse is simply repeated until each promise is described. At the end of each explanation is a prayer that will guide you in confessing the promise. You can repeat these prayers word for word or be creative and pray as the Holy Spirit leads.

Be sure to insert the name of your child in the blanks provided in the sample prayers. You might want to actually write your child's name throughout this book. If you have more than one child, you should get a book for each child, and let each book be an individualized memorial your son or daughter will treasure for years to come. Also, at the end of the book you will find a section for writing prayers God gives you, additional scriptures to declare over your child, impressions you receive from the Holy Spirit, and praise reports when God brings the victory.

Personally I am very careful to record every word that God speaks to me, as well as every prophetic dream. I have learned the importance of pondering the details of these inspired insights for many years afterward and praising God in advance for their fulfillment. So I felt it would be extremely important for you to keep not only a written account of what God *has already said* concerning your children but also to record what God speaks to you *personally*.

However you use this resource, turn every page with a heart full of expectation and hope. This book could be much more than just a blessing; it could be the pivot on which the future of your family turns. I pray that after you've gone through it, you will look back and see such a transformation in your family, you will want to tell everyone that standing on the promises of God really does change things.

IMPARTING THE PROMISES

Not only is it important to pray the sixty-five promises in this book, but you also should find appropriate times to lay hands on your children as you confess these promises over them. God will show you the perfect place and time. You can do it subtly, as if you are just expressing love with a touch, and let the promise ring silently in your heart. Or you can do it openly, especially if your child is fully receptive and cooperative to receiving prayer.

Hebrews 6:1–2 lists the "laying on of hands" as one of six foundational doctrines of the church. It is a biblical practice, often used when praying for healing and in the ordination of elders. Interestingly, the first recorded instance of the "laying on of hands" involved the blessing of children. In Genesis 48:16 we find Jacob laying hands on his grandsons, Ephraim and Manasseh, and praying, "The Angel who redeemed me from all evil, bless the lads."

The "Angel" Jacob referred to was "the Angel of the LORD," something theologians call a Christophany—an appearance of the Lord Jesus Christ prior to His fleshly incarnation. Jacob wrestled with this "Angel" all night long, finally declaring, "I have seen God face to face" (Gen. 32:30; see also Hosea 12:3–4). This was the God of Abraham, Isaac, and Jacob in a bodily form—the One who prospered Jacob and preserved him through all the seasons of his life. To this "Angel of the LORD" Jacob insisted, "I will not let You go unless You bless me!" (Gen. 32:26). God responded, the blessing was granted, and Jacob's name was changed to Israel—because he had struggled with God and with men and prevailed.

Many years later Jacob was hoping to perpetuate this blessing by passing it on to his grandchildren. So he confessed this expectation over their lives with the laying on of hands. This was not a starchy ritual performed with special ecclesiastical garments in a religious location. It was very real and down-to-earth—a private ceremony in a simple family gathering that resulted in a powerful impartation.

Consequently there was an invisible blessing that remained with those two grandsons the rest of their lives, manifesting in very visible and tangible ways. This event was so important, so pivotal, so multigenerational in its impact that it landed Jacob among "the heroes of the faith" recorded in Hebrews 11. Isn't that an attention grabber?

You need to also consider this: Jacob did not have any written, scriptural promises on which to base his faith. His primary motivation was the record of how God had perpetuated the blessing in his own family line: from his grandparents, Abraham and Sarah, to his parents, Isaac and Rebekah, and then into his own life. Because his ancestors had walked in covenant with God, Jacob expected to be blessed and to be a conduit of that blessing to his offspring. If Jacob, with his limited information, could effectively pray over his grandchildren, how much more should we be able to seek God with high expectations? We have a much greater basis for our faith—the entire history of God's intervention on earth in both the Old and New Testaments.

Jacob is not our only example in this area; Jesus prayerfully laid hands on children as well (Matt. 19:13–15)—and He is our chief role model. If the Son of God did it, we should too. I can't help but wonder if in Matthew 19 the Lord confessed over those children some of the promises discussed in this book. If He did, the promises certainly had their impact. I wish we knew the "rest of the story"—what those children became and what great potential was awakened in their lives just because Jesus laid His hands on them and blessed them.

What about your children? What great potential and purpose can be released in their lives if you follow Jacob's—and the Lord's—example of praying over your offspring with the laying on of hands? You will never know until you try.

Waiting on the Promises

It would be so nice to be able to say that God's promises are always fulfilled immediately. That's just not the case. Sometimes God does respond right away, but often we have to "earnestly contend for the faith" over a period of time (Jude 3, KJV). Those who seek to apprehend God's promises must be ready to "fight the good fight of faith" (1 Tim. 6:12). They must daily war against all the doubts and fears that so quickly cloud the mind and hinder us from "possessing our possessions." (See Obadiah 17.)

God gave the Promised Land to the children of Israel, but they still had to fight in order to obtain what was rightfully theirs. And so it is with you and your seed. Hebrews 11:33 says it is "through faith" that promises are obtained. But the chapter makes it clear that this is usually a process that can take some time. Just look at some of the heroes of the faith it mentions.

+ Noah waited 120 years and endured much rejection and ridicule for his promise to come to pass.

+ Abraham and Sarah waited twenty-five years for their promise to come to pass while they watched their aging bodies become increasingly less capable of fulfilling God's pledge.

+ Joseph waited thirteen years for his promise to come to pass, enduring a series of devastating betrayals and disappointments before Pharaoh promoted him to a position of authority in Egypt.

No wonder Scripture encourages us to be followers (or imitators) of "those who through faith and patience inherit the promises" (Heb. 6:12). Patience is simply stick-to-itiveness; it is holding on to the promises until they manifest, enduring all the disheartening and frustrating setbacks that may come.

During this interim—between the promise and its fulfillment—we are simply called to "wait on the LORD." However, doing this does not mean we become lazy or abandon all personal effort. Probably the best definition of this spiritual discipline is this: *abiding peacefully, prayerfully, patiently, passionately, and persistently in God's presence, looking to the future with expectancy and hope.*

Waiting on God involves perseverance in prayer, yet it is also a willingness to accept God's timing on the matter. Those who embrace this heart attitude maintain an underlying trust that the Father will ultimately watch over His Word to perform it—when it is most advantageous and most effective to do so. There are key passages in the Bible that share the wisdom, value, and necessity of "waiting on God." Here are some of the best:

> Wait on the LORD; be of good courage, and He shall strengthen your heart; wait, I say, on the LORD!
> —PSALM 27:14

> Rest in the LORD, and wait patiently for Him…
> —PSALM 37:7

> I wait for the LORD, my soul waits, and in His Word I do hope. My soul waits for the LORD, more than those who watch for the morning—yes, more than those who watch for the morning.
> —PSALM 130:5–6

> But those who wait on the LORD shall renew their strength; they shall mount up with wings like eagles, they shall run and not be weary, they shall walk and not faint.
> —ISAIAH 40:31

So go ahead. Spread your "eagle wings" and soar. Ask God to help you see things from a higher perspective. Don't exhaust yourself batting the air like a sparrow; glide like an eagle. Let the wind of the Spirit carry you.

Most importantly, if at all possible make a quality decision to love and enjoy your children where they are—while you still are waiting for God to take them to the place they need to be. As you pass through this intermediate phase, you may want to implement the wisdom Diana Loomans shares in her wonderful poem reminiscing on her role as a parent:

> If I had my child to raise over again.
> I'd finger paint more, and point the finger less.
> I would do less correcting and more connecting.
> I'd take my eyes off my watch and watch with my eyes.
> I would care to know less and know to care more.
> I'd take more hikes and fly more kites.
> I'd stop playing serious and seriously play.
> I would run through more fields and gaze at more stars.
> I'd do more hugging and less tugging.
> I would be firm less often and affirm much more.
> I'd build self-esteem first, and the house later.
> I'd teach less about the love of power
> And more about the power of love.[5]

I agree! We need to concentrate on teaching and modeling "the power of love." And we need to "behold by faith" that which cannot be seen— the oak tree in the acorn—prayerfully celebrating the expected outcome as we wait for our "seed" to germinate and grow. Instead of reminding God often of your child's shortcomings, praise Him for the desired outcome—the final product, the "tree of righteousness," which surely is "the planting of the Lord" (Isa. 61:3).

"Blessed are all those who wait for Him" (Isa. 30:18).

The Lord Is Building Your House

So there it is! The foundation has been laid. Now you're ready to build—but remember to always acknowledge God's role in the process. The first verse of Psalm 127 (a chapter mentioned often in this book) says it so well—"Unless the LORD build the house, they labor in vain who build it." So invite God now to be the manager of your "family construction project." He will gladly comply, for He has already declared, "The curse of the LORD is on the house of the wicked, but *He blesses the home of the just*" (Prov. 3:33, emphasis added).

God makes Himself very clear in this verse—He *will* bless the home of the righteous. So proclaim this promise over your house with certainty and confidence. Boldly approach God's throne with a Jacob-like attitude in prayer, crying out, "I will not let You go, Lord, until You do this—until You bless my home and until You bless my offspring. You are the God of Abraham, Isaac, and Jacob. You have plans that stretch from generation to generation. I believe that Your best belongs to my seed. I claim a great breakthrough, in Jesus's name." (See Genesis 32:26; Matthew 22:32.)

When this breakthrough comes, be sure to contact us by mail or e-mail and share your praise report. We love you, and we're praying that God will truly bring forth a miracle for your family!

By which have been given to us
exceedingly great and precious promises…
—2 PETER 1:4, MKJV, EMPHASIS ADDED

Promise [noun]—a declaration that one will do
or refrain from doing something specified; a legally
binding declaration that gives the person to whom it
is made a right to expect or to claim the performance
or forbearance of a specified act[6]

1
LIFE

I call heaven and earth as witnesses today against you, that I have set before you life and death, blessing and cursing; therefore choose life, that both you and your descendants may live; that you may love the LORD your God, that you may obey His voice, and that you may cling to Him, for He is your life and the length of your days; and that you may dwell in the land which the LORD swore to your fathers, to Abraham, Isaac, and Jacob, to give them.
—DEUTERONOMY 30:19–20

FIRST, THIS PASSAGE can be seen as a promise of a long and prosperous physical life. (See Psalm 91:14–16.) But more importantly, it refers to "life" in the mental, emotional, and spiritual sense. Anger, pride, lust, depression, fear, rebellion—these attitudes will take you and your children away from God's best for your lives. A home dominated by these attitudes is very dark and full of "death" indeed! When parents "choose life," they tend to walk in attitudes that are the polar opposite: love, humility, selflessness, joy, faith, and obedience to God. These life-giving attitudes of the heart are then passed on to their children, and the life of God embraces them also.

PRAYER DECLARATION

Lord, I claim this promise from Deuteronomy 30. Because I choose to live for truth and for God, I believe spiritual life will be passed to my child. I pray that he/she will continue the family tradition of choosing life and be filled with the very life of God. In doing so, _____ will escape the destructive results of a life of sin. I confess that the life-giving attributes of God's nature—love, joy, peace, righteousness, and goodness—will fill our home, our lives, and our relationship. Yes, I choose life for myself and for my offspring. In the name of Jesus, amen (let it be so)!

2

OBEDIENCE

I call heaven and earth as witnesses today against you, that I have set before you life and death, blessing and cursing; therefore choose life, that both you and your descendants may live; that you may love the LORD your God, that you may obey His voice, and that you may cling to Him, for He is your life and the length of your days; and that you may dwell in the land which the LORD swore to your fathers, to Abraham, Isaac, and Jacob, to give them.
—DEUTERONOMY 30:19–20

WHEN WE AS believers choose life, that automatically involves choosing obedience. On the other hand, if we disobey God, we are choosing death. This is simple to understand; the Bible doesn't mince words on this issue. God warned Adam and Eve in the beginning, "Of every tree of the garden you may freely eat; but of the tree of the knowledge of good and evil you shall not eat, for in the day that you eat of it you shall surely die" (Gen. 2:16–17).

When Adam and Eve chose disobedience, they chose death—and passed the curse of death on to their offspring. Those who choose life walk in obedience to God. In doing so, they pass the legacy of life and obedience on to their seed. You've heard the old saying, "Like father, like son." That's the way it works.

PRAYER DECLARATION

Lord, I claim this promise from Deuteronomy 30. I refuse the spiritual death that results from a life of sin; instead, I choose life. I choose righteousness. I choose to walk in obedience to Your Word and Your will. In response, I believe You will cause a spirit of obedience to rest upon _____ . Instead of the curse of death, he/she will inherit a legacy of life—physically, mentally, emotionally, and spiritually—and obediently walk in it all the days of his/her life. In the name of Jesus, amen (let it be so)!

CIRCUMCISION OF THE HEART

And the LORD your God will circumcise your heart and the heart of your descendants, to love the LORD your God with all your heart and with all your soul, that you may live.
—DEUTERONOMY 30:6

CIRCUMCISION IS THE surgical removal of the male foreskin, usually performed shortly after birth. It is a symbol of God "cutting away" from our hearts the "covering" of fleshly attitudes that prevent us from loving and serving Him.

Often we trust in mere instruction and discipline to effect this change in our children. In this verse God is promising to do it supernaturally. Convincing a child through logic and reason is nowhere near as powerful as when that child has an encounter with God that transforms him or her from within. Praise God, the Most High pledges to do that very thing (Rom. 2:28–29).

PRAYER DECLARATION

Lord, I claim for my child a circumcised heart, that You will "cut away" the worldliness, the carnality, and the sensuality that could otherwise corrupt him/her. I acknowledge that this is a promised divine deliverance, a supernatural act of God, and not something I can force by mere religious instruction. I trust You, Lord, to work this awesome, internal transformation in _____ and give him/her a circumcised heart. In the name of Jesus, amen (let it be so)!

4

LOVE FOR GOD

*And the L*ORD *your God will circumcise your heart and the
heart of your descendants, to love the L*ORD *your God with
all your heart and with all your soul, that you may live.*
—DEUTERONOMY 30:6

ONCE A PERSON'S heart is circumcised, the potential is awakened in him to passionately love the heavenly Father. Romans 5:5 says, "The love of God has been poured out in our hearts by the Holy Spirit who was given to us." So this is evidently a work of God.

God promises that those He "circumcises" will love God with *all* their hearts. When this truly happens, children will automatically be attracted to those things God loves—the things that have eternal value. This impartation of love is so important that Jesus even climaxed His ministry by praying that the Father's love would indwell all new covenant believers (John 17:26). If He prayed this over us, we should certainly pray it over our children.

PRAYER DECLARATION

*Lord, I admit that only You can awaken love for the things of God in
my child's heart. I trust You to do that. I believe _____
will not only love You but will also love the things You love such
as truth, righteousness, and kindness. I believe _____
will be a very loving child—loving family, loving others in the body
of Christ, and loving the lost of this world who have not yet found
their way. Yes, I confess that the love of God will be poured into the
heart of my child. In the name of Jesus, amen (let it be so)!*

5

COVENANT RELATIONSHIP

Therefore know that the LORD your God, He is God, the faithful
God who keeps covenant and mercy for a thousand genera-
tions with those who love Him and keep His commandments.
—DEUTERONOMY 7:9

A COVENANT IS AN agreement between two or more parties, each binding himself to fulfill certain obligations. When we surrender our hearts to the Lord Jesus Christ, we enter a covenant relationship with Him. He in turn obligates Himself to always be with us, forgive us of our sins, fulfill His promises, and preserve us unto eternal life.

This covenantal arrangement overflows to our offspring also. Of course, they must surrender to God in order to receive the fullness of all the covenantal blessings and benefits, but this verse implies that they are automatically on a certain level of covenant connection with God— simply because their parents are already walking with God. Want proof? Remember what God said to Noah, "Behold, I establish My covenant with you *and with your descendants after you*" (Gen. 9:9, emphasis added). The God of Noah is our God. The way He felt then is surely the way He feels now.

PRAYER DECLARATION

Lord, I confess that I am in a covenant relationship with You, and
I believe my descendants are as well. I am committed to You, and
You are committed to me. I believe You will honor our relationship
by committing Yourself also to the welfare of my child in body, soul,
and spirit. I believe You will grant _____ grace to walk
in a covenant relationship with You and prosper all the days of his/
her life. In the name of Jesus, amen (let it be so)!

6

MERCY

Therefore know that the LORD your God, He is God, the faithful God who keeps covenant and mercy for a thousand genera- tions with those who love Him and keep His commandments.
—DEUTERONOMY 7:9

MERCY IS COMPASSION shown especially to those who have engaged in criminal behavior. In a sense, we have all been criminals, for we have all broken God's laws. Titus 3:5 says God saves us, not because of "works of righteousness" but because of "His mercy." According to Deuteronomy 7:9, God stores up a reservoir of mercy for our seed also, so when they need it, His divine compassion will overflow their lives.

God promised to preserve David's dynasty forever. If his offspring sinned, they would be chastened, but divine mercy would protect the Davidic throne. When Solomon, David's son, petitioned God to bless the temple at its dedication, he reminded the Lord of His promise that "sure mercies" would hover over the seed of David (Isa. 55:3). God responded by sending such intense glory in the temple that the priests could not even enter (2 Chron. 6:41–7:3). This event illustrates how powerfully God honors parents who serve Him. If He did it for David's seed, He will do it for ours—and God's mercy and glory will overflow in their lives.

PRAYER DECLARATION

Lord, I believe You store up mercy for the offspring of the righteous. If my child errs in life, I believe Your mercy will guide him/her back to You to find forgiveness, cleansing, and restoration. Lord, have mercy upon _____ and deliver him/her in every trial, temptation, failure, or disappointment. I appeal to You, O Father of mercies, to make my child a vessel of mercy on whom You will pour out Your glory and through whom You will express Your mercy to others. In the name of Jesus, amen (let it be so)!

7

SALVATION

*Believe on the Lord Jesus Christ, and you will
be saved, you and your household.*
—Acts 16:31

A mazingly this promise was not made to a seasoned saint but to an unsaved man on the verge of suicide. God had just responded to the praise of Paul and Silas by sending an earthquake that shook open the doors of the prison in which they were held. Assuming the prisoners had escaped, the Philippian jailer was about to kill himself.

"But Paul called with a loud voice, saying, 'Do yourself no harm, for we are all here.' Then he called for a light, ran in, and fell down trembling before Paul and Silas. And he brought them out and said, 'Sirs, what must I do to be saved?' So they said, 'Believe on the Lord Jesus Christ, and you will be saved, you and your household'" (Acts 16:28–31).

If a man just introduced to the faith could receive this divine commitment, how much more those who have fought the good fight of faith for years! We who believe have a legal right to claim our families for the kingdom, for the King has pledged, "I will contend with him who contends with you, and I will save your children" (Isa. 49:25). Salvation means deliverance, so God is promising to deliver our children.

PRAYER DECLARATION

Lord, based on these promises I claim salvation for my child. I believe You will contend with any satanic force that may be contending with our family. You are the God of an army of angels that have been "sent forth to minister for them who shall be heirs of salvation" (Heb. 1:14, KJV). So dispatch them, Lord, to protect and defend my child. I pray You will save _____ from the deception of this world and grant him/her all the benefits of salvation. In the name of Jesus, amen (let it be so)!

8

A LEGACY OF INTEGRITY

The righteous man walks in his integrity; his children are blessed after him.
—PROVERBS 20:7

THE WORD *INTEGRITY* means firm adherence to a code of moral values. Men and women of integrity have a passion for honesty, sincerity, and truth. Such traits tend to produce success and prosperity and normally result in a life well lived.

There are two primary reasons descendants of such people are blessed. First, adherence to such a values system creates stability in the home, a healthy atmosphere conducive to raising healthy children. Second, they leave a legacy of integrity; their lifestyle of integrity with all of its benefits is passed down to generations following.

Two other versions express this same passage in pleasant terms. The Contemporary English Version explains, "Good people live right, and God blesses the children who follow their example." And the Living Bible concludes the verse by saying, "It is a wonderful heritage to have an honest father."

PRAYER DECLARATION

Father God, I thank You first for the grace to walk in integrity that I may pass this heritage on to my child. When deceit is more convenient, let me be honest instead. When compromise entices, let commitment surge within me. When hypocrisy stalks me, let sincerity guard my soul. When immorality woos my mind, let my heart remain pure and my standards strong. Help me to be a role model for my child. Give me the grace to be strong in these areas of character and then transfer this legacy of inner strength to _____ with all of its benefits and blessings. In the name of Jesus, amen (let it be so)!

PROVISION

I have been young, and now am old; yet have I not seen the
righteous forsaken, nor his descendants begging bread.
—PSALM 37:25

WHAT A COMFORT to know that if we as parents walk in righteousness, God will see to it that our offspring have an ample supply of necessary natural provisions! Certainly we can find exceptions to this in a world full of poverty and lack. However, generally speaking, we can expect this to be the case.

There are extreme examples in Scripture that should build our faith. What about God giving Joseph such divine insight that the needs of his family were met during seven years of famine? What about the manna that came down from heaven during Israel's wilderness journey? What about the widow and her son, who were on the verge of starvation when Elijah prophesied that a meal barrel and a cruse of oil would never fail to produce? Of course, there is no more powerful example than Jesus multiplying the loaves and fishes and feeding the multitudes. If He took care of His people then, He can certainly take care of us and our children now.

PRAYER DECLARATION

O God, I confess over my family that You are the Lord our Provider. I believe You will always make ample provision for my child. Even during hard times, I pray that _____ will always have sufficient food and shelter. Moreover, I praise You for leading _____ into the right career and giving him/her the best job opportunities and the highest wages possible. I declare before Your throne that my seed will never have to beg. Favor will go before _____, and golden doors of opportunity will continually open before him/her, both naturally and spiritually. In the name of Jesus, amen (let it be so)!

WORLD CHANGERS

Who is the man who fears the LORD? He will instruct him
in the way he should choose. His soul will abide in pros-
perity, and his descendants will inherit the land.
—PSALM 25:12–13, NAS

THIS PROMISE EVIDENTLY means more than just acquiring real estate. On a higher level, "inheriting the land" speaks of having prominence and influence in order to transform individuals or society as a whole with the values and character of God's kingdom. This can happen for believers' offspring on a local or global level; they can "inherit" everything from neighborhoods to nations. (See Psalm 2:8; Isaiah 54:3.)

A good example is Martin Luther King Jr. Not only were his parents strong Christians, but also both his father and grandfather were preachers. When Martin was around the age of seventeen, the "ministry mantle" passed to him. Though he never held a political office or owned large masses of real estate, Martin Luther King Jr. "inherited the land" in a more profound way. As he selflessly began promoting racial equality in Alabama, God began promoting him to a place of international prominence. If you have surrendered your life to the Lord Jesus Christ, expect Him to awaken in your son or daughter a similar potential of being a world changer and a history maker.

PRAYER DECLARATION

Lord, I pray that _____ will "inherit the land," that he/she will be a person of influence in this world. I believe that through my child You will mold and shape the values of his/her generation in a positive and powerful way. I also confess that _____ will inherit the land in a literal sense, ruling and reigning with You in the kingdom of God to come, forever and ever. In the name of Jesus, amen (let it be so)!

11

THE OUTPOURING OF GOD'S SPIRIT

For I will pour water on him who is thirsty, and floods on the dry ground; I will pour My Spirit on your descendants, and My blessing on your offspring.
—Isaiah 44:3

THE MOST IMPORTANT experience any child can have is a real, personal encounter with the living God. It is not enough for children to merely witness the reality of God in the lives of their parents; they must experience it for themselves. If we thirst after God, the Father promises to do that—to pour out the living water of His Spirit upon their lives.

God has promised that He will be "with the generation of the righteous" (Ps. 14:5). Therefore, if we "thirst for righteousness" (Matt. 5:6) and walk in the "paths of righteousness" (Prov. 2:20), God promises to be with our offspring, influencing their lives with His outpoured presence. Certainly a child must make a personal decision claiming Jesus as his Lord in order for the Savior to actually dwell in his heart, but until that spiritual rebirth takes place, our decision to serve God will apparently cause His Spirit to be with them in a special way, drawing them to Himself.

Prayer Declaration

Lord, I thirst for You. I pray that Your living water will fill my soul and flow through my child as well. I confess that my son/ daughter will never be like a desert but will blossom with the beauty of the Lord and bear fruit for Your kingdom. Because I thirst for righteousness, I trust that Your presence will be with my child always, guarding, guiding, and instructing him/her in every situation. As _____ begins seeking You and drinking of Your presence, I pray that this spiritual water will become in him/ her a well of water springing up into everlasting life. In the name of Jesus, amen (let it be so)!

THE OUTPOURING OF GOD'S BLESSING

*For I will pour water on him who is thirsty, and floods on the dry ground;
I will pour My Spirit on your descendants, and My blessing on your off-
spring. They will spring up among the grass like willows by the watercourses.*
—ISAIAH 44:3–4

IN THIS PASSAGE God promises to pour out two things on the children of those who thirst after Him: His Spirit and His blessing. A blessing is any benefit from God that causes happiness, fulfillment, or wholeness in a person's life. When God pours out His blessing on our children, we can expect their needs to be met physically, materially, mentally, emotionally, and spiritually.

Blessed children are happy children. They do not have fragmented personalities and are not empty-hearted. They are fulfilled and contented, walking in God's purpose. They tend to then pass the blessing on to others that the blessing of God might fill the earth.

PRAYER DECLARATION

Lord God, I thank You by faith for Your blessing descending on my child. Let it pour down like the rain of heaven. I believe that this divine blessing will be evidenced in every area of my child's life—physically, materially, socially, emotionally, mentally, and spiritually. Your Word declares that "the blessing of the Lord makes one rich, and He adds no sorrow with it" (Prov. 10:22). Thank You for enriching _____ with all the benefits You have promised in Your Word, crowning his/her life with the best that heaven can provide. In the name of Jesus, amen (let it be so)!

SPIRITUAL GROWTH: UNIQUENESS AND EXCELLENCE

For I will pour water on him who is thirsty, and floods on the dry ground;
I will pour My Spirit on your descendants, and My blessing on your off-
spring. They will spring up among the grass like willows by the watercourses.
—ISAIAH 44:3–4

WHEN PARENTS WALK in truth, their relationship with God provides "streams of living waters" (John 7:38, NIV) that constantly flow through the lives of their children. This nurtures them spiritually and helps them grow. Children are constantly "watered" by the example of their parents and the training they receive, and they should constantly grow in God as a result. In fact, living trees never stop growing. Scripture says John the Baptist and even the Lord Jesus "grew" and became "strong in spirit" when they were children (Luke 1:80; 2:40).

God's people should expect the same for their children. As our key verse puts it, the offspring of the righteous will "spring up…like willows by the watercourses." Willow trees, because of their drooping branches, can remind us of our need to be humble before God—to bow before Him submissively and adoringly. In this passage our seed are characterized this way. But the willow could also speak of children who are unique and extraordinary, who excel in their gifting and calling in life—children who stand out in the crowd, as willow trees stand out in contrast to mere grass.

PRAYER DECLARATION

Lord, I believe _____ will spring up before You and be humble, submissive, and adoring toward You all his/her days. I confess that because You promised to pour out Your Spirit and Your blessing on my offspring, it will come to pass. _____ will ever grow in the things of God, nourished by the constant flow of the river of God's presence in his/her life. In the name of Jesus, amen (let it be so)!

DIVINE INSTRUCTION

All your children shall be taught by the LORD, and
great shall be the peace of your children.
—ISAIAH 54:13

THIS VERSE IS literally talking about the offspring of New Jerusalem, the eternal city of God. Yet God identifies New Jerusalem as "the bride, the Lamb's wife" (Rev. 21:9). So on a prophetic and symbolic level, a promise to the children of New Jerusalem is a promise to the children of those who make up the bride that this city represents.

How comforting it is to know that God Himself will instruct our children! We can go only so far in helping them to understand the mysteries of the kingdom of God. We can fill their minds with information, but only God can fill their hearts with revelation—which He promises to do in this passage. He will grant them insight into human character and teach them how to be successful in every area of life.

PRAYER DECLARATION

Lord, I believe that no one can come to You unless the Holy Spirit draws him. I also believe that when this happens, Your Spirit intends to lead that person—step-by-step—into all truth. I claim this kind of divine instruction for my child. I confess that the "Spirit of wisdom" (Eph. 1:17) will open _____'s eyes to the truth and reveal to him/her the "deep things of God" (1 Cor. 2:10). I also believe You will teach _____ how to have fruitful and godly relationships and a successful life in every way. In the name of Jesus, amen (let it be so)!

GREAT PEACE

All your children shall be taught by the LORD, and
great shall be the peace of your children.
—ISAIAH 54:13

PEACE IS CALMNESS of mind and heart. It may not mean a life free
from stress, but it certainly means maintaining a tranquil attitude
even in midst of traumatic circumstances. Jesus is called "the Prince of
Peace" (Isa. 9:6). When He's invited to reign in a person's heart, He
brings many gifts, including peace. He promised His followers, "My
peace I give to you.... Let not your heart be troubled" (John 14:27, MKJV).

In our key passage God promises an overflow of His peace into the
lives of our offspring. This means much more than just human emotion.
The Bible describes it as "peace...in the Holy Spirit" (Rom. 14:17) and
"the peace of God, which surpasses all understanding" (Phil. 4:7, MKJV).
No wonder Isaiah 54:13 calls it "great" peace. In a strife-filled world, how
needed is this pledge from the lips of the Almighty!

PRAYER DECLARATION

Lord, I believe, as Your Word promises, that You will extend peace
to me "like a river" (Isa. 66:12) and that this peace will flow over
the soul of my child as well. I pray that _____ will be
preserved from the things that can create stress, strife, and anxiety
in our hearts. May _____ always maintain "peace with
God" (Rom. 5:1), a harmonious relationship with You, and may the
"peace of God" (Phil. 4:7) always abide within him/her. Your Word
declares that You are the God of peace. I pray that _____
will so completely yield to Your peaceful nature that he/she even
becomes a means of passing this wonderful gift on to others—
fulfilling the call to be a "peacemaker" in the earth (Matt. 5:9). In
the name of Jesus, amen (let it be so)!

IMPARTED RIGHTEOUSNESS

But the mercy of the LORD is from everlasting to everlasting on those who fear Him, and His righteousness to children's children.
—PSALM 103:17

THIS VERSE PROMISES that God's righteousness—not just humanly attained righteousness—passes to the offspring of those who fear the Lord. This wonderful "gift of righteousness" also comes in response to faith (Rom. 5:12–21). "Abraham 'believed God, and it was accounted to him for righteousness'" (Gal. 3:6; see also Rom. 4:19–25). Certainly Abraham's offspring did not automatically inherit this imparted righteousness from God just by virtue of their natural birth, but they did inherit the knowledge of how to access this wonderful opportunity. And so it is with our children.

While the adherents of most world religions strive to reach the elusive goal of righteousness through works, Christian parents can teach their offspring to set their faith on the cross, where Jesus was made to be "sin for us, that we might become the righteousness of God in Him" (2 Cor. 5:21, see also Rom. 10:9–10).

PRAYER DECLARATION

Lord God, I pray first that my child will understand the righteousness that comes as a gift from God. I also pray and believe that he/she will access this righteousness by faith and respond by living righteously before You all of his/her days. May _____ "hunger and thirst for righteousness" (Matt. 5:6) and, as a result, be "filled with the fruits of righteousness" (Phil. 1:11). In the name of Jesus, amen (let it be so)!

17

HOPE FOR RESTORATION

There is hope in your future, says the LORD, that your children shall come back to their own border.
—JEREMIAH 31:17

THIS WAS INITIALLY a reference to the children of Israel, who were captives of war, carried away into the bondage of Babylon. Enslaved in a foreign nation, they longed to be free and to see their children return one day to the Promised Land. God testified in this passage that their hopes would be fulfilled.

This scripture can also be claimed in a spiritual sense concerning backslidden children of godly parents. Though their offspring have been "carried away" into the "bondage" of a worldly lifestyle and "enslavement" to sin, committed parents can trust that their offspring will be brought back to the "border" of a spiritual land of promise: a place of blessed and fruitful relationship with the Most High God.

On a higher level, this promise is applicable to all of us. It celebrates the hope we have of returning to the perfection of the original paradise state—returning to the "border" of the Garden of Eden and the intimacy with God that our foreparents knew.

PRAYER DECLARATION

Lord, I confess that as long as there is a God in heaven, there is hope. If _____ ever strays from Your will, or if this has already happened, I confess that my child will always come back to the "boundary" of the truth. I claim that _____ will be blessed to dwell in a spiritual land of promise, a land filled with both the promises in Your written Word and any living word promises You have spoken over his/her life. Most importantly, I confess that _____ will be restored to the perfection of paradise when You return in glory. In the name of Jesus, amen (let it be so)!

ANOINTED FRUIT BEARERS

Your wife shall be like a fruitful vine in the very heart of your house, your children like olive plants all around your table.
—Psalm 128:3

THERE ARE THREE primary aspects to this wonderful promise. This verse tells us that the children of the righteous will be:

1. *Fruit bearers.* Olive trees bear fruit. Symbolically this means the children of God's people will be fruit bearers. They will bear the fruit of the Spirit (the character of God), the fruit of good works, and the fruit of souls won into the kingdom of God. (See John 4:36; Galatians 5:22–23, Ephesians 5:9; Philippians 4:17.)

2. *Spiritually hardy.* Olive trees are also very hardy plants that can grow well in rough and rocky terrain. So the children of the righteous should be very capable— through the grace of God—to handle the rough, rocky territory they face in life.

3. *Anointed.* Olive oil is a strong, biblical symbol for the anointing of the Holy Spirit. The anointing is even referred to as "the oil of gladness" (Ps. 45:7; Heb. 1:9) and "the oil of joy" (Isa. 61:3). So God is promising that the children of the righteous will be producers of the anointing—that they will manifest the power of God as they minister the truth to others.

PRAYER DECLARATION

Lord God, on the basis of Psalm 128:3, I pray that my child will be like an olive plant at my table, that _____ will bear much fruit, and be a blessing to others and a praise to God in the earth. If he/she faces rough and rocky places in life, I believe my child will be able to endure with Your help. I confess that the "oil of gladness" (the anointing of the Holy Spirit) will flow through _____ powerfully to extend the kingdom of God in this world. I speak these things knowing that Your Word will not return void. It will accomplish what You have declared. In the name of Jesus, amen (let it be so)!

19

HOLY UNTO THE LORD

*For the unbelieving husband is sanctified by the wife, and
the unbelieving wife is sanctified by the husband; otherwise
your children would be unclean, but now they are holy.*
—1 CORINTHIANS 7:14

THIS IS A comforting promise, especially in divided homes where only one parent is serving God. First, the unbelieving spouse is sanctified (set apart for God) by the commitment of the believing partner. This does not mean that person's sins are forgiven even when no repentance is present. It simply means the person is consecrated to God by the prayerfulness and faith of the saved spouse. It seems that God is "legally" released to deal more profoundly with that person as a result.

In like manner, the children of this union are also automatically considered holy unto the Lord (separated from the world and dedicated to the Father). In order for the children to receive the full benefits of salvation, God will certainly require them to personally consecrate themselves to God, but because of their parent's commitment the path has already been cleared for them—and the way has been made much easier.

PRAYER DECLARATION

Lord God, I declare that my son/daughter is holy unto the Lord, dedicated to You, and consecrated to Your purposes. I believe You will honor my commitment to You by separating _____ from the world and drawing him/her to Yourself. I pray and believe _____ will be kept from the defilement and corruption that is so rampant in the earth today. Instead, I confess that by grace my child will have a passion for holiness and be pleasing in Your sight. In the name of Jesus, amen (let it be so)!

PROCLAIMERS OF GOD'S WORD

"As for Me," says the LORD, "this is My covenant with them: My
Spirit who is upon you, and My words which I have put in your
mouth, shall not depart from your mouth, nor from the mouth of
your descendants, nor from the mouth of your descendants' descen-
dants," says the LORD, "from this time and forevermore."
—ISAIAH 59:21

VISION IS GENERATIONAL. God imparts a certain revelation of His
Word to a man or woman of faith. Then, for it to reach maximum
effectiveness, the same truth is often passed to that person's offspring.

John and Charles Wesley shook the world in their day with the revelation of the true gospel. However, the message did not originate with
them. They gained many of their insights and passion for God from
Samuel and Susanna Wesley, the God-loving parents who planted the
seed of truth within the brothers' hearts. Wouldn't it be wonderful if
your child ended up as fruitful in God's work as these two giants of the
faith? If it happened in the Wesley home, it can happen in yours.

PRAYER DECLARATION

Lord God, I thank You for all the truths You have revealed to me.
I declare that these truths will not end with me. Part of the legacy
I pass to my son/daughter are the God-given insights that have
transformed my life. Lord, You prayed for Your disciples, saying,
"[Father,] I have given them the words which You have given Me"
(John 17:8). I pray the same for _____, that he/she will
receive the same revelation of truth You have given me. I pray that
my child will be personally transformed by this insight, that he/she
will always live according to the truth, and that _____ will
be a powerful voice of truth in a world full of spiritual deception.
In the name of Jesus, amen (let it be so)!

UNDER ANGELIC PROTECTION

*Take heed that you do not despise one of these little
ones, for I say to you that in heaven their angels always
see the face of My Father who is in heaven.*
—MATTHEW 18:10

J ESUS EVIDENTLY WAS referring to *all* children here, not just those of
believers. First, He warned against any cruel treatment of "little ones."
Second, He revealed that one or more angels are assigned to each child and
that these heavenly beings consult with the Father concerning any adverse
situations in that child's life. Apparently these guardian angels are ever
ready to request divine intervention or retribution. If this is true for *all* children, how much *more* the children of God's people! (See Daniel 12:1–2.)

Hebrews 1:14 explains that angels are "ministering spirits sent forth
to minister" for the heirs of salvation. That means they work behind
the scenes to bring forth God's best in everything that pertains to you,
including your children. Jesus confided that if He asked, the Father
would have sent twelve legions of angels to defend Him (Matt. 26:53).
Certainly He can do the same for any child committed to His care.

PRAYER DECLARATION

*Lord God, You are the Lord of hosts, the God of an army of angels
who are poised and ready for battle. I confess that at least one angel is
assigned to constantly watch over _____, to ensure divine
protection and provision in his/her life. According to Your Word, just
one angel defeated the entire Assyrian army (2 Kings 19:35). So one
angel in my child's life is sufficient to bring deliverance in every area
of need. Yet I believe that there are many ministering spirits actively
engaged in ministering to our family—that we might inherit all the
benefits of salvation. I praise You that this very thing is taking place
right now. In the name of Jesus, amen (let it be so)!*

CLINGING TO GOD

I call heaven and earth as witnesses today against you, that I have set before
you life and death, blessing and cursing; therefore choose life, that both you
and your descendants may live; that you may love the LORD your God, that
you may obey His voice, and that you may cling to Him, for He is your life
and the length of your days; and that you may dwell in the land which the
LORD swore to your fathers, to Abraham, Isaac, and Jacob, to give them.
—DEUTERONOMY 30:19–20

HAVE YOU EVER seen a scared or troubled child clinging to Mommy's skirt or Daddy's pants with all his might? This is the picture I get when I read this promise. As parents grow in their relationship with God, more and more they assume the posture of clinging to the Creator in times of trouble and in the midst of a very wicked world. This impresses the minds of their children, often compelling them to take the same stance. People of this world tend to cling to a rope that unravels, and they often perish as a result—mentally, emotionally, and even physically. God's offspring cling to an unbreakable chain of hope in God's promises. At the end is the "anchor of the soul" (Heb. 6:19) that goes beyond the veil of time.

PRAYER DECLARATION

Lord God, I first confess that I not only believe in You, but I also
cling to You. In times of difficulty my intentions are to hold on
to You with all my might. I pray You will awaken this depth of
dependency in my son/daughter. Instead of clinging to the things
of the world for fulfillment and satisfaction, may _____
always cling to You—with a tenacity that will never let go. I con-
fess that this kind of spiritual stick-to-itiveness will be the prevailing
attitude of my child's heart all the days of his/her life. In the name
of Jesus, amen (let it be so)!

CREATED FOR GOD'S GLORY

Fear not, for I am with you; I will bring your descendants from the east, and gather you from the west; I will say to the north, "Give them up!" and to the south, "Do not keep them back!" Bring My sons from afar, and My daughters from the ends of the earth—everyone who is called by My name, whom I have created for My glory; I have formed him, yes, I have made him.
—Isaiah 43:5–7

WHEN WE READ these verses, we should lift our eyes toward God in worshipful awe. God actually refers to our offspring as His sons and His daughters. In other words, God is saying, "Because they belong to you, they belong to Me. Because you have named My name over their lives, I claim them as My own."

God also asserts that our offspring have been created for His glory. The world system would like to seduce our seed to spend their lives giving glory to that which has little or no value. Declare over your child that his talents or her abilities will never be wasted in vain pursuits, but that his or her life will be invested only in that which gives praise, honor, and acclaim to the Creator.

PRAYER DECLARATION

Lord, I pray that You will gather _____ unto Yourself and deliver him/her from all the entrapments of this world. Because of the covenant we share, all that I have belongs to You. So I confess Your name over _____, and I believe You will claim him/her as Your own. I trust You to prevent _____ from devoting his/her life to that which would glorify human achievement alone. Instead, awaken such divinely inspired purpose in my child that glory ascends to You from his/her life. In the name of Jesus, amen (let it be so)!

AN ENDURING HOUSE

Then it shall be, if you heed all that I command you, walk in My ways, and do what is right in My sight, to keep My statutes and My commandments, as My servant David did, then I will be with you and build for you an enduring house, as I built for David, and will give Israel to you.
—1 KINGS 11:38

ALTHOUGH THIS PARTICULAR promise was originally spoken to an individual (Jeroboam, the son of Nebat), it is applicable to any parents who strive to keep God's commandments. First, God is saying that the family line will endure—it will continue from generation to generation.

Second, God is pledging to the righteous, "Your children will have a spirit of endurance. They will fight the good fight of faith. They will be tenacious in the face of rejection or opposition. They will persevere in living the truth, when others are weak and succumb to the influence of an evil world." Enduring families and enduring children—that's what this twofold promise is all about!

PRAYER DECLARATION

Lord God, my passion is to heed Your commandments and walk in Your ways. Therefore, I have a right to expect the fulfillment of this promise. In an age of great instability in many families, I believe that I will have "an enduring house." I pray that a spirit of endurance will also rest upon my child, that _____ will always be able to "endure temptation" and "endure hardship as a good soldier of Jesus Christ" (James 1:12; 2 Tim. 2:3). I confess by faith that _____ will be able to "run with endurance" (Heb. 12:1) the race set before him/her and successfully make it all the way to heaven. In the name of Jesus, amen (let it be so)!

INCREASE

The LORD shall increase you more and more, you and your children.
—PSALM 115:14, KJV

I N THIS VERSE God promises "increase" but doesn't specify the particular areas. Most likely this divine pledge should be realized in every area of our lives and the lives of our children—ever-increasing peace and joy, ever-increasing wisdom and knowledge, ever-increasing effectiveness and fruitfulness, ever-increasing intimacy with God and sensitivity to His will, and even ever-increasing material prosperity.

Referring to certain churches under his care, the apostle Paul said, "I planted, Apollos watered, but God gave the increase" (1 Cor. 3:6). In like manner parents are called to plant seeds of truth in the lives of their children, then water the seeds with much love, but God is the One who brings forth increase—from "faith to faith" (Rom. 1:17), from "strength to strength" (Ps. 84:7), and from "glory to glory" (2 Cor. 3:18)!

PRAYER DECLARATION

O Lord of increase and abundance, I pray that You will be mindful of all the seeds of truth I have planted in my son/daughter. I pray these seeds will be watered by much love—both mine and Yours— and that they will germinate, grow, and bring forth great increase in every area of my child's life. Lord Jesus, just as You increased in wisdom, stature, and favor with God and man, so let it be for my child. Yes, I pray, believe, and confess that _____ will increase "with the increase that is from God" (Col. 2:19). In the name of Jesus, amen (let it be so)!

STRONG CONFIDENCE

In the fear of the LORD there is strong confidence, and
His children will have a place of refuge.
—PROVERBS 14:26

THE GOOD NEWS Translation puts the above passage this way: "Reverence for the LORD gives confidence and security to a man and his family." Many people lack confidence in life. Instead they are intimidated by people, paralyzed by the past, perplexed by the present, afraid of the future, and constantly battling insecurities and feelings of inferiority. Not so for those who fear the Lord, for as the maxim states, "The man or woman who fears God has nothing left to fear."

If we are submitted to the headship of Christ, in Him "we have boldness and access with confidence" (Eph. 3:12). Most would agree that this means we have access into the presence of the Father, but it may also mean access into our future destiny and purpose. Awakening in our offspring this kind of tenacious faith and bold assurance is very much a part of the spiritual legacy we are called to impart.

PRAYER DECLARATION

Lord, I claim that an atmosphere of the fear of the Lord will permeate my home and hover over my family—a loving devotion that trembles at Your holiness and melts in Your presence. I declare that You are Lord of this home. I honor and reverence You to the highest degree. I pray this heart attitude of the fear of the Lord will always abide within my child, and that as a result _____ will walk in strong confidence all the days of his/her life. I confess that he/she will never be intimidated by people, afraid of circumstances, or overwhelmed by challenges. Instead, may _____ always have a sense of unfailing security in You and in the grace You provide. In the name of Jesus, amen (let it be so)!

REFUGE FROM THE STORM

In the fear of the Lord is strong confidence: and
his children shall have a place of refuge.
—Proverbs 14:26, kjv

THE FEAR OF the Lord is the highest degree of reverence for God. Parents whose hearts are inclined this way build a refuge for their children in a world that often disrespects and disregards God. When we infuse our children's minds with the fear of the Lord, we teach them that they are accountable to God, and we awaken in them a desire to be acceptable in His sight. This builds confidence in our offspring that they can be righteous in God's sight and receive His provision and protection.

We know ominous clouds are on the horizon spiritually. Very dark things are predicted over this planet. Such prophetic insight can cause even believers to be concerned about what their children might face. Yet we know that our Savior is "a refuge from the storm" (Isa. 25:4). Though tumultuous times are ahead, the Prince of Peace will come and make wars "cease to the ends of the earth" (Ps. 46:9). No wonder the psalmist was rejoicing as he concluded, "The LORD of hosts is with us; the God of Jacob is our *refuge*" (v. 11, emphasis added). No better refuge can be found!

PRAYER DECLARATION

Lord God, I declare that I fear You, and I have endeavored to instill this reverential awe in my child. We honor You and exalt You to the highest place in our lives. We are filled with awe at Your greatness, Your holiness, and Your power. Because of this, I believe You will respond by building a wall of defense around us. I claim divine protection for my child in every area of life, especially as we approach the last days. Though this world is filled with danger and deception, I confess that _____ will always have a place of refuge in You. In the name of Jesus, amen (let it be so)!

FREEDOM FROM CAPTIVITY

Now it shall come to pass, when all these things come upon you, the blessing and the curse which I have set before you, and you call them to mind among all the nations where the LORD your God drives you, and you return to the LORD your God and obey His voice, according to all that I command you today, you and your children, with all your heart and with all your soul, that the LORD your God will bring you back from captivity, and have compassion on you, and gather you again from all the nations where the Lord your God has scattered you.
—DEUTERONOMY 30:1–3

FROM THE PERSPECTIVE of the new covenant, this promise is especially for families who have fallen away from the Lord yet have repented and returned to Him. God pledges to deliver them from "captivity"—loosing them from the error of their pasts. However, this is not just for the formerly backslidden. We can all relate to this promise— for at times we all "fall away" from the goal of walking in perfect faith, obedience, and love. As a result, we become "captivated" by fear, doubt, depression, anger, resentment, and many other kinds of bondage. But Jesus came to "proclaim liberty to the captives" (Isa. 61:1).

The great mystery of the matter is this: having conquered the great enemies of the human race (sin, Satan, the curse, death, and the grave), the Son of God ascended victoriously to heaven. During that pivotal event this captain of our salvation "led captivity captive" (Eph. 4:8). In other words, He captivated, or put under His dominion, anything that could potentially captivate us or our children. The more we return to the Lord—dedicating ourselves to the things of God—the more He will activate this part of our inheritance and loose us from any captivating influence.

Prayer Declaration

Lord God, who bought our freedom through Your death, burial, and resurrection, I recommit myself and my child to You. We have, at times, strayed from Your perfect will through our attitudes and actions, and ended up in some kind of captivity. I repent for myself and for _____. I pray You will have compassion on us and deliver us from every area of bondage. I fully expect that You will do these things because You paid such an awesome price to set us free. Now it is our privilege and responsibility to respond. Through the weapons of warfare that You have given us, we bring "every thought into captivity to the obedience of Christ" (2 Cor. 10:5). I refuse to accept any stronghold of negative or worldly thinking in me or in _____. I claim the blood of Jesus, the name of the Lord, and the Word of God—weapons that are "mighty in God" (2 Cor. 10:4), toppling every area of resistance in both of us. As Scripture declares, "Evil people will surely be punished, but the children of the godly will go free" (Prov. 11:21, NLT). I claim that freedom in our family. In the name of Jesus, amen (let it be so)!

29

COMPASSION

Now it shall come to pass, when all these things come upon you, the blessing and the curse which I have set before you, and you call them to mind among all the nations where the LORD your God drives you, and you return to the LORD your God and obey His voice, according to all that I command you today, you and your children, with all your heart and with all your soul, that the LORD your God will bring you back from captivity, and have compassion on you, and gather you again from all the nations where the Lord your God has scattered you.
—DEUTERONOMY 30:1–3

COMPASSION IS SYMPATHETIC love—love that feels the pain of another person. We have all faltered and failed in life and suffered the consequences. But according to this verse, if we return to God, He will have compassion on us and on our children.

The God of Abraham also promised that if His people returned to Him, they and their children would be "treated with compassion" by those who took them captive (2 Chron. 30:9). One great display of compassion was when Pharaoh's daughter found the baby Moses in a basket floating down the Nile. "She had compassion on him," and he became her adopted son (Exod. 2:6). If this dual promise is given to erring yet repentant believers, how much more will it manifest for those who are consistent in serving God!

PRAYER DECLARATION

Lord God, I repent of all my shortcomings and areas of failure. I return to You with all my heart and recommit myself to Your purpose. I believe You will honor Your Word, showing compassion to me and to my child _____. I also believe that You will even cause others to show compassion toward us, because we are submitted to You. In the name of Jesus, amen (let it be so)!

DOING WELL

Therefore know this day, and consider it in your heart, that the LORD
Himself is God in heaven above and on the earth beneath; there is
no other. You shall therefore keep His statutes and His command-
ments which I command you today, that it may go well with you and
with your children after you, and that you may prolong your days
in the land which the LORD your God is giving you for all time.
—DEUTERONOMY 4:39–40

I N 2 KINGS 4 we read about a notable woman in Shunem who reverenced God. She offered the prophet Elisha a room in her home. God rewarded her with a miracle. Though childless, she conceived and bore a son. Later on, the child fell in the field crying, "My head," and died shortly after. The Shunammite woman rushed to find the prophet, expecting God to use him to restore her child.

Gehazi, Elisha's servant, encountered the woman first and asked, "Is it well with you?...Is it well with the child?" Amazingly her response was, "It is well" (2 Kings 4:26)! She dared to confess what she believed God would do—and it happened. The child was raised back to life.

We should speak similar words of faith over our children. Even if it appears they are nearly "dead" spiritually or doing badly in certain areas, we should still dare to say, "*It is well*," putting our faith in God's ability to change circumstances and hearts.

PRAYER DECLARATION

Lord, I confess that You are God in heaven and on earth, and
I seek to obey Your commandments. Therefore, I believe that it
will "go well" with me and with my child _____ as You
promised—in every area of life. I believe this so completely that
even in challenging or difficult times in my child's life, I dare to con-
fess by faith, "It is well." In the name of Jesus, amen (let it be so)!

FEARFULLY AND WONDERFULLY MADE

For You formed my inward parts; You covered me in my mother's womb. I will praise You, for I am fearfully and wonderfully made; marvelous are Your works, and that my soul knows very well.
—PSALM 139:13–14

UNQUESTIONABLY, PSALM 139 is one of David's most beautiful psalms—a masterpiece of God-inspired truth. It celebrates God's involvement in the formation, both naturally and spiritually, of a child in the womb. This unique passage is a declaration of God's watchfulness over all His chosen ones who are yet to be born. Since God's people normally dedicate their children to God even prior to birth, the promises in this psalm apply to them even more powerfully.

In the passage above, David claimed that the Most High actually formed his "inward parts." That could be referring to the organs of the body that are hidden from view or to the soul and spirit (the human personality and spiritual capacity of an individual). It's probably referring to both. So one of God's "marvelous works" is the implanting of a predetermined personality that must be perfected and a potential spirituality that must be awakened in a child that is yet to be born. As parents we are called to assist in this process.

In a subsequent verse David made another profound declaration, saying, "Your eyes saw my substance, being yet unformed. And in Your book they all were written, the days fashioned for me, when as yet there were none of them" (v. 16). So apparently there is a providential plan in our children's lives that unfolds like a huge red carpet, stretching all the way from eternity past to eternity future. According to 2 Timothy 1:9, God has given His people a "purpose and grace…in Christ" before the world began. We should declare this promise over our children, that they are truly part of a divine plan and that God will give them sufficient grace to fulfill their part. Contemplating these truths should cause us to conclude, as David did, that "such knowledge is too wonderful" (v. 6).

Prayer Declaration

Lord God, I believe that my child has been "fearfully and wonderfully made." I confess that Your hand covered _____ in the womb and that Your hand will cover him/her all the days of his/her life. I believe that You have formed my child's "inward parts" (the potential personality and inner, spiritual capacity). I rest in this truth and pray that You will continue to involve Yourself in the soulish and spiritual development of my child, just as You involved Yourself in his/her physical development in the womb. Finally, I confess that the future of my child is not up to chance; You have a plan for _____. I praise You for causing it to unfold perfectly according to Your pleasure and predetermined purpose. Such knowledge is so wonderful; it moves my heart to worship You, O Lord of the past, present, and future. I declare victory in advance. In the name of Jesus, amen (let it be so)!

LONGEVITY

*Today I am explaining his laws and teachings. And if you
always obey them, you and your descendants will live long
and be successful in the land the LORD is giving you.*
—DEUTERONOMY 4:40, CEV

LEGEND HAS IT that Ponce de Leon discovered Florida in 1513 while seeking the Fountain of Youth. Eight years later, instead of finding the key to longevity, he died at the hands of the Calusa Indians. Ironically, a search for extended life actually led to an early death.

Now, as the baby boomer generation moves into the status of senior citizens, the search to reclaim youthfulness continues. A new industry is flourishing with products designed to slow the process of aging. By implementing nutritional and lifestyle changes, some people may be able to temporarily fight back the hands of time, but eventually all human beings will fall prey to this persistent stalker.

Our key scripture above shares one key to longevity: keeping God's commandments and abiding in His teachings. The Bible gives at least five other ways of securing a long life. They include:

+ Honoring your father and mother, "that your days may be long" (Exod. 20:12)

+ Seeking wisdom, for "length of days is in her right hand" (Prov. 3:16)

+ Setting your love upon God and knowing His name, for He promises, "With long life I will satisfy him" (Ps. 91:16)

+ Fearing the Lord, for "the fear of the LORD prolongs days, but the years of the wicked will be shortened" (Prov. 10:27)

- Rehearsing and displaying God's Word in your home, "that your days and the days of your children may be multiplied...like the days of the heavens above the earth" (Deut. 11:21)

Of course, the most excellent promise is immortality, which we receive when we set our faith on the Lord Jesus Christ, for "he who believes in the Son has *everlasting life*" (John 3:36, emphasis added).

Prayer Declaration

Lord God, I make a commitment to obey Your commandments, to seek wisdom, to set my love upon You, and to fill my home with Your Word—that my days and the days of my child may be long upon the earth. More importantly, I confess that my faith is set upon You, Jesus, that I might inherit the gift of eternal life. May this gift of all gifts also be poured out on my son/daughter, that _____ and I might live forever in Your presence. In the name of Jesus, amen (let it be so)!

SUCCESS

Today I am explaining his laws and teachings. And if you
always obey them, you and your descendants will live long
and be successful in the land the LORD is giving you.
—DEUTERONOMY 4:40, CEV

SUCCESS SEMINARS HAVE abounded in recent years. Those leading these sessions tout many "keys to success": a good self-image, positive thinking, a proper education, a neat appearance, eloquent speech, showing genuine interest in others, and so forth. There is certainly some value in all these keys, but they often leave out the most important secret to success.

God admonished Joshua, "This Book of the Law shall not depart from your mouth, but you shall meditate in it day and night, that you may observe to do according to all that is written in it. For then you will make your way prosperous, *and then you will have good success*" (Josh. 1:8, emphasis added).

Daily confessing Scripture, pondering its true meaning, keeping its commands, and claiming its promises—these are some of the greatest keys to success that exist for us and for our children. As Psalm 112:1–2 says, "How joyful are those who fear the LORD, and delight in obeying his commands. Their children will be successful everywhere" (NLT).

PRAYER DECLARATION

Lord God, I declare that I honor Your Word—that it will always
be in my mouth. I will meditate on it day and night, and I will
always seek to live within its boundaries. I believe this will bring
good success in my own life and in the life of my son/daughter. I
now pass on this legacy of a Word-based lifestyle to _____.
It will cause my child to be successful everywhere he/she goes. In
the name of Jesus, amen (let it be so)!

DELIVERANCE

*Though hand join in hand, the wicked shall not be unpun-
ished: but the seed of the righteous shall be delivered.*
—Proverbs 11:21, kjv

I T WAS THE first Passover in the land of Goshen. In the early evening
thousands of Israeli men dipped hyssop in lamb's blood and applied it
to the upper doorpost and two side posts of their homes. The destroyer
would visit Egypt that night, and every firstborn son would die. But
God promised His people, "When I see the blood, I will pass over you"
(Exod. 12:13). The next day wails were heard all over the land. The Egyptian sons were slain, and great grief, like swelling waters from the Nile,
flowed through the streets. But the Israelite sons were delivered.

The men of Israel had no idea their act of applying lamb's blood was
prophetic in nature. They were actually making the sign of the cross,
prophesying of another Lamb yet to come who would deliver His people
from death—not only physically but spiritually and eternally as well. In
a way similar to this grand biblical event in Exodus, we must mark our
homes, claiming the blood of Jesus as a protective covering over our seed.
As many young people succumb to the deadly influences of a society that
is becoming increasingly evil, it is our responsibility as parents to make
a prayerful, prophetic statement in our homes that heaven will honor.

Prayer Declaration

*Lord God, there are many deadly influences around my child. The
world's system, which is dominated by the evil one, will destroy the
souls of children who are unprotected. But I claim the blood of Jesus
over my home and my offspring. I believe _____ will be
preserved from evil for "the eye of the Lord is on those...who hope
in His mercy, to deliver their soul from death" (Ps. 33:18–19). In
the name of Jesus, amen (let it be so)!*

FOOLISHNESS REMOVED

Foolishness is bound up in the heart of a child; the
rod of correction will drive it far from him.
—Proverbs 22:15

MOST BIBLE PROMISES are given with conditions. This verse in Proverbs is a prime example. In order for foolishness to be driven from the hearts of our children, we must be willing to wield "the rod of correction"—but what is that rod? Is it just physical punishment for shortcomings? That may certainly be part of it. As the adage goes, "Spare the rod and spoil the child." (See Proverbs 23:14.)

Sometimes, though, a rod can represent words—especially words spoken with authority. A good example is Isaiah 11:4, a prophecy that the Messiah would "strike the earth with the rod of His mouth." (See also Proverbs 14:3.) Jesus certainly was no easygoing preacher; He exposed hypocrisy, sin, and rebellion whenever He preached.

Those who love God welcome His words of correction, for they keep us from the contaminating influence of a foolish world. In the end our children will love us also, if we are careful to discipline them this way— correcting wrong behavior and leading them in the path of wisdom. David, in his famed Twenty-Third Psalm, told the Shepherd-God, "Your rod and Your staff, they comfort me" (v. 4). Similarly, the "rod of correction" wielded by loving parents should also be a "comfort" to any child— for their words point the way to a life that pleases God.

PRAYER DECLARATION

Lord God, how foolish this world is with its ungodly agendas and its refusal to surrender to the truth. Your Word says that even the "thought of foolishness is sin" (Prov. 24:9, KJV). I repent of it all. I ask You to cleanse me and my child of all worldly influence. I recognize that "foolishness is bound up in the heart" of my child because of an inherited fallen nature. But Your Word can remove it and drive it far from him/her. I pray that _____ will not succumb to the foolishness of the carnal nature but will instead embrace the wisdom of God and receive a new nature. I make a commitment to lovingly discipline my child when it is needed so that the "rod of my mouth" will lead him/her in the way of truth and bring comfort to my child, now and forevermore. In the name of Jesus, amen (let it be so)!

ROOTED IN THE TRUTH

*Train up a child in the way he should go, and when
he is old he will not depart from it.*
—PROVERBS 22:6

EARS AGO I visited a friend whose hobby was horticultural studies (which he insists is much more than mere gardening). At the entrance of his home was a small tree I didn't recognize. "What's that?" I asked. "A weeping cherry tree," he responded. Surprised, I said, "I've heard of a weeping willow but not a weeping cherry tree. Don't the branches of a cherry tree grow straight up? These are hanging down."

My friend then proceeded to explain how he caused the tree's branches to turn downward. When the tree was just a sapling, he split the trunk, turned one side upside down, and fused the two pieces back together. He explained that this confused the tree's "internal thinking," so that later on when it "thought" it was growing up, it was really growing down.

That happens with children too. Sometimes through the bad influence of peers, authority figures, and even carnally minded parents, a child's thinking gets "twisted" around at an early age. Consequently these individuals often equate adulthood with sensual indulgence and sinful excess. As they get older, they tend to mimic that behavior. The sad truth is that when they think they are finally growing up, they are actually "growing down."

Of course, if the negative is true, the positive is true also. Good role models persist for a lifetime. Parents who have good, moral lives are training their children by example. They are guarding their offspring with a lasting impression of the truth that will cause them to grow up healthy and normal. Yes, we need to train the minds of our children in biblical truths and moral laws, but more than that, we need to live those truths and laws before their impressionable eyes every day.

Prayer Declaration

Lord God, when You came to earth, You trained us by sharing many truths that challenge the world's way of doing things. But more than that, You lived out those concepts before us. Help me to properly train my child, not only in words but also with my example. Let both leave a lasting impression on my child's heart and mind, so that when _____ is grown, he/she will not depart from the right way of living. I claim this promise and expect it to come to pass. In the name of Jesus, amen (let it be so)!

37

PRESERVED FROM TROUBLE

*They shall not labor in vain, nor bring forth chil-
dren for trouble; for they shall be the descendants of the
blessed of the LORD, and their offspring with them.*
—ISAIAH 65:23

THIS VERSE IS foretelling the glory of the new creation. God also
promises that He will make Jerusalem "a rejoicing, and her people
a joy" (v. 18). No longer will "the voice of weeping" (v. 19) be heard. Life
will be stable. God's elect will "long enjoy the work of their hands" (v.
22). All of nature will be reconciled: for "the wolf and the lamb shall feed
together" (v. 25). The land will be called "Beulah," meaning married—for
all things will be married to God in an overflow of celestial splendor.

The Holy Spirit also foretells that the people of the new earth will
not "labor in vain, nor bring forth children for trouble" (v. 23), for "they
are the seed of the blessed of the LORD, and their offspring with them" (v.
23, KJV). Though this promise is primarily futuristic, the "blessed of the
LORD" can confess even now: "I did not bring my child into this world for
trouble, to be overcome by trials, temptations, or tribulations. By faith
I declare that he/she will have a peaceful, fruitful, and successful life."

PRAYER DECLARATION

*Lord, I confess that I did not bring _____ into this
world to be destroyed by the troubling things that abound here. As
a family we may face temptations and trials, but we know You will
be our "strength in the time of trouble" (Ps. 37:39), a "refuge in
times of trouble" (Ps. 9:9), and You will even "preserve" us "from
trouble" (Ps. 32:7). I declare by faith, in the end, that any trouble-
some thing encountered in life will only serve to help God's purposes in us to achieve final fulfillment. In the name of Jesus, amen
(let it be so)! (See also Proverbs 11:8; 12:13.)*

PROVIDENTIAL CARE

They shall not labor in vain, nor bring forth children for trouble;
for they shall be the descendants of the blessed of the LORD, *and*
their offspring with them. It shall come to pass that before they
call, I will answer; and while they are still speaking, I will hear.
—ISAIAH 65:23–24

THIS PASSAGE PROPHESIES of the glorious reign of Jesus Christ in the new world that is yet to come. In that era God will be so intimately involved with His people that He will automatically anticipate anything they might request of Him. In one translation of verse 24, God even says, "I will answer their prayers before they finish praying" (CEV). That's just the way a loving Father is.

Good parents do something similar almost daily. A concerned mother knows that when her daughter comes home from school, she's going to want her favorite snack when she gets home, so she prepares in advance. As soon as the girl says, "Mommy…," the mother respond with, "It's on the countertop," and a smile breaks out on the child's face. If earthly parents can be that way with their offspring, how much more the omniscient, omnipotent, omnipresent God! He knows what we need before we do. Such compassionate oversight is not just for the kingdom to come; it is a promise that both we and our offspring can claim right now.

PRAYER DECLARATION

Lord God, I confess that my child and I are blessed and that You are watching over us constantly—ever anticipating our future needs. You promised that before we call upon You, the answer will be sent. I claim that kind of divine oversight for my son/daughter. May _____ never face anything in life without Your grace and provision being supplied ahead of time and manifesting right when it is needed. In the name of Jesus, amen (let it be so)!

VESSELS OF PERFECT PRAISE

But when the chief priests and scribes saw the wonderful things that He did, and the children crying out in the temple and saying, "Hosanna to the Son of David!" they were indignant and said to Him, "Do You hear what these are saying?" And Jesus said to them, "Yes. Have you never read, 'Out of the mouth of babes and nursing infants You have perfected praise'?"
—MATTHEW 21:15–16

AFTER JESUS CLEANSED the temple of the moneychangers, the blind and lame came to Him and were healed. The children present began worshipping the Lord, shouting, "Hosanna to the Son of David!" This greatly offended the religious leaders, who were steeped in self-righteousness. Jesus responded to them by quoting this verse from Psalm 8.

It is quite amazing that top-rated theologians in Jesus's day were oblivious to the power of God manifesting before their eyes. The children, however, were not blinded by religious traditions and doctrines. They were not protecting some position of power. They were just ecstatic at what God was doing and willing to respond with joy.

Far too often the praise that goes on in our churches is linked to mindless ritual, tainted by religious pride, and devoid of passion. Real praise is not practiced, polished, professional, or performed. It is simple, sincere, humble, spontaneous, and full of passion for the Most High. Jesus proclaimed that God perfects this kind of praise in children.

PRAYER DECLARATION

Lord God, You deserve to be praised with all our heart, mind, soul, and strength. I pray that You will make _____ a true vessel of praise. May he/she always react to the blessings of God with great gratitude and heartfelt adoration flowing toward Your throne. Yes, Lord, I confess that my child will be a true worshipper all the days of his/her life. In the name of Jesus, amen (let it be so)!

STRENGTH TO CONTINUE

The children of Your servants will continue, and their
descendants will be established before You.
—PSALM 102:28

O N ONE LEVEL this verse speaks of the continuation of the family line from generation to generation. On another level it speaks of an attitude of the heart. So many people lack diligence; they are unwilling to stick with a task until it's done. They don't hang in there when the going gets tough. But in this verse God promises His servants that their offspring will be quite the opposite. Why?

Often the attitude is inherited. When children witness stick-to-itive-ness in their parents, they tend to "catch it." Most godly people have plenty of trials to pass through, but if they are truly committed, they do just that—they pass through. They keep going. The Bible urges God's people to "continue in the grace of God," "continue in the faith," "continue in His goodness," and "continue earnestly in prayer" (Acts 13:43; 14:22; Rom. 11:22; Col. 4:2). Jesus summed up this need for continuance with this challenge, "If you abide in My word, you are My disciples indeed" (John 8:31, MKJV). Let these passages be descriptions of you and your child.

PRAYER DECLARATION

Lord God, You remain the same yesterday, today, and forever. I pray that You will so infuse my family with Your nature that we also never change in our commitment to the truth. Give me grace first as a parent to continue in Your Word—always abiding by its commands and claiming its promises. Then let this legacy pass to my child. I pray that _____ will be consistent in his/her relationship with You, and that he/she will continue in the grace of God, in the faith, in Your goodness, and in earnest prayerfulness. In the name of Jesus, amen (let it be so)!

41

STABILITY

*The children of Your servants will continue, and their
descendants will be established before You.*
—Psalm 102:28

To be "established" means to be made firm or stable. This world is quite the opposite; it is a very unpredictable place. One day everything can be wonderful, and the next day disaster can strike. Notable past events easily prove this: Pearl Harbor, 9/11, and Hurricane Katrina, just to name a few. But no matter what happens, those who walk with God can be steady, unafraid, and undeterred concerning their purpose.

Many promises in Scripture confirm this. One stands out: "But the Lord is faithful, who will establish you and guard you from the evil one" (2 Thess. 3:3). This passage reveals the mystery behind our security. We can expect stability in our lives and the lives of our children simply because God is stable. He is unchanging. He is faithful to the principles that rule His kingdom, to those who love Him, and to their offspring. Our seed are established before God. He constantly keeps our children under His surveillance and is always ready to intervene on their behalf.

PRAYER DECLARATION

Lord, thank You for showing me the source of stability. I declare over my household, "God is our refuge and strength, a very present help in trouble. Therefore we will not fear, even though the earth be removed, and though the mountains be carried into the midst of the sea" (Ps. 46:1–2). Yes, even in times of cataclysmic upheaval we can trust in You and be unmoved. I claim this kind of stability for myself and for my child. I believe You will "establish peace for us," "establish the work of our hands," and establish our "hearts blameless in holiness before our God…at the coming of our Lord Jesus Christ" (Isa. 26:12; Ps. 90:17; 1 Thess. 3:13). In the name of Jesus, amen (let it be so)!

SPIRITUAL MIGHT

Praise the LORD! Blessed is the man who fears the LORD, who
delights greatly in His commandments. His descendants will be
mighty on earth; the generation of the upright will be blessed.
—PSALM 112:1–2

THIS IS A power promise if ever there was one. Weak parents tend to
raise weak children. But parents who fear the Lord—that's another
story! By yielding to God's Spirit (called the "Spirit of might" in Isaiah
11:2), these parents conquer sin, self, and the spirit of the world. What a
legacy to pass on! The children of such parents know, "If Dad and Mom
can overcome that way, I can too!" Thus they are far more capable of
doing great things in life and impacting the world in a mighty way.

Orville and Wilbur Wright had strong Christian parents, and look
at how they influenced the earth through the development of air flight.
And what about Billy Graham, who is certainly one of the most influen-
tial Christian leaders of this generation? He had strong Christian parents. After receiving the baton of consecrated faith from them, he passed
it on to his offspring as well, and they are still impacting this world with
the gospel. May the same thing take place in your family!

PRAYER DECLARATION

Lord, I live before You in godly fear, revering Your holiness and
standing in awe of Your majesty and power. My passion is to
keep Your commandments. I delight in obeying Your Word. So,
according to this promise, I can expect my child to do mighty
works for the kingdom of God and change this world in a pow-
erful way. Father, I pray that You will awaken the "Spirit of might"
in _____ and strengthen him/her "with might" through
Your Spirit "in the inner man" (Eph. 3:16). In the name of Jesus,
amen (let it be so)!

WEALTH

Praise the LORD! Blessed is the man who fears the LORD, who delights
greatly in His commandments. His descendants will be mighty on
earth; the generation of the upright will be blessed. Wealth and
riches will be in his house, and his righteousness endures forever.
—PSALM 112:1–3

THE GOOD NEWS Translation of this passage puts it his way, "Happy is the person who honors the LORD, who takes pleasure in obeying His commands. The good man's children will be powerful in the land; his descendants will be blessed. His family will be wealthy and rich."

Sought for its own sake, wealth can be corruptive, but when sought for the kingdom's sake, it can be very beneficial. When God sees that our priorities are right, He desires to pour out power, wealth, riches, prosperity, and success—for us and for our children.

Deuteronomy 8:18 reveals the primary reason God gives the seed of the righteous "power to get wealth." He does this so He may establish the covenant made with their foreparents. So if we serve God, there should be an overflow of wealth to our children. As the Puritan preacher Cotton Mather put it, "Religion begat prosperity."[1]

The Almighty knows that His work requires financing: churches must be built, missionaries must be supported, television and radio programs must be produced, books and tracts must be published, and the poor must be given much-needed assistance. To accomplish these worthy goals, the Lord of all empowers certain individuals in the body of Christ to prosper materially and then passes the same blessing on to their offspring. Like Abraham of old, they are blessed to be a blessing (Gen. 12:2).

PRAYER DECLARATION

Lord God of heaven and earth, I confess that the earth is Yours
and the fullness of it. All the silver is Yours and all the gold.

All the cattle on a thousand hills belong to You. So I claim this promise of wealth for my son/daughter, but not just for his/her benefit personally. More importantly, I claim this promise so that _____ will be used by You, Lord, to finance Your work and the great harvest of souls that will come in these last days. I also pray, Lord God, that wealth will never corrupt my child, but that on the contrary he/she will always seek the wealth of Your people, just as Mordecai did so many years ago (Esther 10:3, KJV). Once this blessing manifests, may _____ always remember to help the poor and those in need, for this is the heart of God. In the name of Jesus, amen (let it be so)!

RICHES

Praise the LORD*! Blessed is the man who fears the* LORD*, who delights greatly in His commandments. His descendants will be mighty on earth; the generation of the upright will be blessed. Wealth and riches will be in his house, and his righteousness endures forever.*
—PSALM 112:1–3

THE WORD HOUSE in this passage refers to a person's household or family. Accordingly, the Good News Translation renders verses 2–3 this way: "The good man's children will be powerful in the land; his descendants will be blessed. His family will be wealthy and rich."

There is plenty of evidence that conferring material riches is, at times, very much a part of God's blessing on an individual or a group of people. For example, Abraham was *"very rich* in livestock, in silver, and in gold" (Gen. 13:2, emphasis added). Along with Abraham's far more important spiritual legacy, natural riches were part of the inheritance he passed to his offspring. It is also true that many centuries later Jesus actually became "a curse" (when He died on the cross) so "the blessing of Abraham" could pass to all new covenant children of God (Gal. 3:13–14).

Of course, the greatest riches are spiritual in nature. Jesus called them "true riches" (Luke 16:11). God has promised that His people will inherit the riches of His goodness, glory, grace, and mercy (Rom. 2:4; 9:23; Eph. 1:7; 2:4). Furthermore, James 2:5 asks, "Has not God chosen the poor of this world to be rich in faith and heirs of the kingdom which He promised to those who love Him?" These are the primary riches we should all desire, but both classes of riches—natural and spiritual—are part of the dual legacy that we can pass to our children.

PRAYER DECLARATION

Lord God of the entire universe, all things belong to You. In Your abundant generosity You have promised to meet all our needs

*according to Your riches in glory. I pray first for _____,
that the Word of God will dwell in him/her richly and that he/
she will be filled with the riches of Your mercy, Your goodness,
and Your grace. I believe that _____ will not only be
rich in faith but also rich in good works, as Scripture commands
(1 Tim. 6:18). I also claim natural riches for my child, but not to
the detriment of his/her relationship with You. Let riches increase
in his/her life, but let love for God increase even more, so that
my child, above all, is "rich toward God" (Luke 12:21). Since I
believe You have already purposed to do this, by faith I confess over
_____ the words of 1 Corinthians 4:8, "Now ye are rich"
(KJV). In the name of Jesus, amen (let it be so)!*

REDEMPTION

The LORD did not set His love on you nor choose you because you were more in number than any other people, for you were the least of all peoples; but because the LORD loves you, and because He would keep the oath which He swore to your fathers, the LORD has brought you out with a mighty hand, and redeemed you from the house of bondage, from the hand of Pharaoh king of Egypt.
—DEUTERONOMY 7:7–8

TO BE REDEEMED means to be freed from bondage by means of a purchase price. In this passage God promises redemption to the people of Israel based on the oath He swore to their forefathers. If we are in a covenant relationship with the same God, we can expect similar treatment for our offspring. No matter what "bondage" may be present in our children's lives, we can prayerfully confess that God will redeem them and deliver them with "a mighty hand." Therefore "let the redeemed of the LORD say so" (Ps. 107:2)!

PRAYER DECLARATION

Lord God, I confess that my son/daughter is loosed from all bondage—set free by the precious blood of Jesus. No past, present, or future bondage will ever prevail against _____. The world, sin, deception, satanic enticements, the flesh, even fear of death—none of these things will ever be able to enslave this child who is dedicated to You. I pray that You will always be a deliverer, guardian, and guide to _____, bringing him/her out of any weakness, darkness, or difficult situation of life. I pray that by Your mighty hand You will lead my child into the promised land of his/her destiny. You are the almighty God! There is nothing too hard for You! So I declare redemption over my offspring, believing it will come to pass. In the name of Jesus, amen (let it be so)!

PROPHETIC INSIGHT

"And it shall come to pass in the last days," says God, "that I will pour out of My Spirit on all flesh; your sons and your daughters shall prophesy, your young men shall see visions, your old men shall dream dreams."
—ACTS 2:17

THIS PROPHECY, ORIGINALLY given in Joel 2:28, began its era of fulfillment with the birth of the church on the Day of Pentecost (Acts 2:1–18). It is still coming to pass, because God is still pouring out His Spirit and transforming sons and daughters into His prophets and prophetesses. These terms may sound a little presumptuous to some believers, yet they are very biblical.

Prophetic insight can manifest on several levels. On the most fundamental level a person can be described as prophesying when he or she simply shares the Word of God under the power, guidance, and inspiration of the Holy Spirit. (It is the Holy Spirit who shows a prophetic person whom to speak with, what to say, and when to say it.) This kind of insight can come when a person is preaching from a pulpit, talking with a neighbor in the backyard, or even during times of great opposition (Matt. 10:18–20).

At times God speaks to His people through prophetic words, dreams, or visions, giving them discernment and understanding about certain people or events or their own destiny in God (Num. 12:6; John 10:27). Prophetic knowledge is especially associated with those who have received glimpses into God's future plans and purposes in the earth.

Anyone who can read the Bible has access to divine revelation, but only born-again, consecrated individuals, under the guidance of the Holy Spirit, can properly interpret and propagate the message God seeks to convey. Anyone who has truly accepted Christ as his Savior can be used as a prophetic instrument. The apostle Paul asserted, "You can all prophesy" (1 Cor. 14:31), and that includes you and your offspring who are walking with God.

Prayer Declaration

Lord God Almighty, I pray that according to the promise of Acts 2:17, You will pour out Your Spirit on _____ and awaken a prophetic calling and gift in his/her life. Thank you for manifesting prophetic knowledge in _____ on several levels: first, that he/she will understand Your Word by divine inspiration; second, that he/she will be able to effectively prophesy truth to others by the power and inspiration of the Holy Spirit; and third, that he/she will have great insight into the prophetic events that will unfold in the last days as we near Your return. I pray that You will grant _____ prophetic words, dreams, and visions. Give my child grace to boldly proclaim what he/she receives from You. I confess that these things will happen, all for Your glory and the advancement of Your kingdom. In the name of Jesus, amen (let it be so)!

VISIONS

"And it shall come to pass in the last days," says God, "that I will pour out of My Spirit on all flesh; your sons and your daughters shall prophesy, your young men shall see visions, your old men shall dream dreams."
—ACTS 2:17

VISIONARIES ARE THOSE who receive plans and strategies from God. By faith and by God's power they implement those divine instructions to advance the purposes and kingdom of God in this world. Every generation needs "seers"—people of vision who know by divine inspiration exactly what to do in order to significantly impact individuals, communities, and even nations for the sake of the gospel. There is absolutely no reason we should think adults are the only ones God can use in this way. Acts 2:17 promises that our sons and daughters will have literal visions from God. At an early age Samuel received a vision from God that altered his life dramatically and caused him to emerge as a prophet to his generation (1 Sam. 3).

God still moves on children supernaturally. Sometimes they even receive literal visions from the Almighty. When our son was only about four years old, he surprised us all one morning by blurting out, "Last night I died in my sleep, and Jesus took me to heaven!" Then he began to explain certain details about what he heard and saw. The descriptions were so profoundly deep and the language so mature, we knew it could not be merely the product of a child's imagination. Though our son certainly didn't die, we believe he definitely experienced a night vision from the Lord, a grace-filled glimpse into the celestial world. I pray that God will grant your child supernatural visitations as well!

PRAYER DECLARATION

Lord God Almighty, I confess this promise of vision over my son/ daughter. Thank You for pouring out Your Spirit on _____ *and supernaturally revealing Your plans for his/her life. I pray You will also cause my child's heart to burn with passionate commitment to the holy cause that You place within him/her. Holy Father, I believe You will open my child's spiritual sight, even to the point that he/she will receive actual visions from above in the same way You gave Samuel a supernatural revelation when he was a child. I pray that _____ will never accept a mundane and normal life but will reach out with visionary zeal to embrace the uncommon and God-inspired goals that are a part of Your plan. On the basis of this promise in Acts 2:17 I claim both waking visions and night visions (inspired dreams) for my child, that he/she might be led into the depths of Your purpose and be a champion for the truth in this world. In the name of Jesus, amen (let it be so)!*

48

POWER TO STAND

*The wicked are overthrown and are no more, but
the house of the righteous will stand.*
—PROVERBS 12:7

THIS VERSE SPEAKS of two primary things. First, it implies that a life of righteousness tends to bring stability and long-term growth to a family—the "house" as a whole will stand. Second, it speaks God's promise to the individual offspring: that in times of trouble, disappointment, lack, and even times of oppression and persecution, the seed of the righteous will stand. They will not back down, give up, or waver. They will stand fast, resisting temptation and possessing their God-given inheritance.

This is part of the legacy godly fathers and mothers pass down. When the children of the righteous watch their parents go through tough times—and survive by fighting the good fight of faith and seizing God's promises—they learn to imitate the same tenacious behavior. Example engenders in their hearts the same determination to stand, and the family tradition continues.

PRAYER DECLARATION

Lord God, I believe that my child will stand firm, trusting in the promises of God no matter what he/she faces in life. I confess that _____ will stand against temptation when it entices, stand for the truth when others compromise, and stand in faith when circumstances cause doubt to cloud his/her mind. I pray _____ will be a worshipper and stand in Your holy place (Ps. 24:3). I pray _____ will be an intercessor and "stand in the gap" for others (Ezek. 22:30). Finally, I pray that _____ will never be intimidated by fearful things in life but will "stand still, and see the salvation of the Lord" (Exod. 14:13). In the name of Jesus, amen (let it be so)!

DIVINE HEALTH

*Because you have made the LORD, who is my refuge, even
the Most High, your dwelling place, no evil shall befall
you, nor shall any plague come near your dwelling.*
—PSALM 91:9–10

W HAT DOES IT mean to make the Lord your "dwelling place"? Surely
that is much different than just seeking Him in times of trouble
(getting religious when the heat's on). Rather, it speaks of a 24/7 relationship, having a heart that is always inclined toward heaven.

When God finds people who love abiding in His presence, He promises the reward found in our key scripture. In essence He is saying, "If
you decide to live with Me, then I will decide to live with you. I will be
an invisible presence, abiding in your home, repelling evil, and pouring
out My blessing on everyone under your roof."

The specific promise in Psalm 91:9–10 is divine health—not just the
removal of disease, but also the prevention of it. The passage says it will
not come "near" our "dwelling." Those who live in our homes should
automatically receive the overflow of this blessing. If in 1 Samuel 6 the
household of Obed-Edom was blessed because the ark of the covenant
was placed in his home, how much *more* will your household be blessed
if the divine presence that rested in the ark actually lives within you?

PRAYER DECLARATION

*Lord God, I believe the promise of Deuteronomy 7:15 that You will
take away all sickness from Your people. But better still, I believe
the promise of Psalm 91:10—that no sickness will come near my
dwelling. Thank You for protecting _____ from all disease
and imparting divine health to our family—wholeness in body, mind,
soul, and spirit. You are the Lord our healer (Exod. 15:26), and You
are Lord of our home. In the name of Jesus, amen (let it be so)!*

KNOWLEDGE OF GOD'S WORD

For He established a testimony in Jacob, and appointed a law in Israel,
which He commanded our fathers, that they should make them known to
their children; that the generation to come might know them, the children
who would be born, that they may arise and declare them to their children.
—PSALM 78:5–6

THE WORD TRANSLATED "law" in this passage is the Hebrew word
torah. This is actually a name for the first five books of the Bible:
Genesis, Exodus, Leviticus, Numbers, and Deuteronomy. These foundational books contain much more than the law (a list of commandments
from God). They are full of faith-building stories, wonderful revelations
of the character of God, and prophetic glimpses of what is yet to come.
We have more than five books in the Bible now; we have sixty-six. And
how much more valuable is this treasure today, especially those books
revealing the life of Jesus and the glory of the new covenant!

It is very important that this knowledge be imparted to the next generation. We cannot keep it to ourselves. Thank God for those who have
diligently watched over the preservation of God's Word in centuries
past—such as the scribes of old who carefully handwrote God's Word
one copy at a time, or more recent heroes such as John Wycliffe and
William Tyndale, who first dared to translate the Bible from Latin into
English, the language of the common people. Tyndale was martyred for
his "crime." May we value the price that others have paid, cherish God's
Word, promote it in all that we do, preserve its values, and pass this holy
responsibility on to our seed—that the work of God might continue in
the earth.

PRAYER DECLARATION

Lord God, Your Word is a lamp unto our feet and a light unto
our path. This is such a dark world, full of deception and death.

There are no survivors here except those who discover Your truth and live in it. Help me to transfer to my offspring the correct interpretation of Your Word, and awaken in _____ a deep understanding of truth and a strong appreciation of its value. Help me to live your Word before my child so that he/she receives a living example of how the Word of God should mold our lives. Then empower _____ to walk in my footsteps and be a testimony of truth to the next generation. In the name of Jesus, amen (let it be so)!

HOPE IN GOD

For He established a testimony in Jacob, and appointed a law in Israel, which He commanded our fathers, that they should make them known to their children; that the generation to come might know them, the children who would be born, that they may arise and declare them to their children, that they may set their hope in God, and not forget the works of God, but keep His commandments.
—Psalm 78:5–7

HOPE HAS BEEN defined as desire married to expectation. Tertullian, one of the early church fathers, said, "Hope is patience with the lamp lit."[1] According to our key passage, one of the primary reasons God gave us His Word was to transfer hope to future generations. It is not enough for this soul-warming sunshine to reach the full-grown "trees"; it must shine down to the forest floor and nurture the "saplings" as well.

Life is often unpredictable. At times we may even face what appears to be a hopeless situation—but we are in covenant with the "God of hope," who fills us with "all joy and peace in believing" that we may "abound in hope by the power of the Holy Spirit" (Rom. 15:13).

Though this generation is careening downhill toward a time of tribulation unlike anything the world has ever seen, we have a "blessed hope" (Titus 2:13): the glorious appearing of the Lord Jesus Christ. Scripture promises that when we see Him, "we shall be like Him," and "everyone who has this hope in Him purifies himself, just as He is pure" (1 John 3:2–3). Yes, of all the promises we can pass to our children, this is one of the most important—that Jesus is coming again to establish Himself once and for all as Lord of lords and King of kings, in heaven and on earth!

PRAYER DECLARATION

Lord, I set my hope in You—always and in all things. I declare that there is no hopeless situation. Thank You for giving me the courage to expect Your promises to be fulfilled. This hope is the "anchor" of my soul in stormy seas. By faith I pass this spiritual capacity to my child—the ability to hold on tenaciously to the promises of God, no matter what happens in life. I believe that You will fill _____ with "all joy and peace in believing" that he/she may always "abound in hope" through the power of the Holy Spirit, as we both look forward to that "blessed hope" of Your return, and " the hope of glory" that resides within us. In the name of Jesus, amen (let it be so)! (See Hebrews 6:19; Romans 15:13; Colossians 1:27.)

REMEMBERING GOD'S WORKS

For He established a testimony in Jacob, and appointed a law in Israel, which He commanded our fathers, that they should make them known to their children; that the generation to come might know them, the children who would be born, that they may arise and declare them to their children, that they may set their hope in God, and not forget the works of God, but keep His commandments.
—PSALM 78:5–7

SHARING THE WORD of God with our children prepares them for life. As we tell the story of Adam and Eve, they will understand our fallen state and God's promise of redemption. When they hear of Noah and his family, they will understand that God protects His own. As we tell of Abraham and Sarah, it will build their faith for overcoming impossible situations. As we relate Israel's deliverance from Egypt, they will be convinced that God's power can set them free from any bondage in their lives.

It is so important to impart this knowledge. After the Israelites walked through the Jordan River and possessed the Promised Land, a horrible thing transpired. Judges 2:10–12 says, "When all that generation had been gathered to their fathers, another generation arose after them who did not know the LORD nor the work which He had done for Israel. Then the children of Israel did evil in the sight of the LORD...and they forsook the LORD God of their fathers." This must not take place in your family. Think back on all the works of God that you have witnessed in your own life personally. Share these stories with your child—often. By doing so, you will keep the fire of faith burning from generation to generation.

Prayer Declaration

Lord God Almighty, I praise You for all Your mighty works—those You have accomplished in generations past and those You have wrought during my lifetime. Give me grace to transfer to my child not only the knowledge of these works but also the expectation that You can move in his/her behalf as well. Don't ever let my child forget what You have done. I claim the ever-constant overshadowing of the Spirit of truth upon _____, bringing all of Your works and Your Word to his/her remembrance, that he/she might serve You and be kept from this evil world (John 14:17, 26). In the name of Jesus, amen (let it be so)!

KEEPING GOD'S COMMANDMENTS

*For He established a testimony in Jacob, and appointed a law in
Israel, which He commanded our fathers, that they should make
them known to their children; that the generation to come might
know them, the children who would be born, that they may arise and
declare them to their children, that they may set their hope in God,
and not forget the works of God, but keep His commandments.*
—PSALM 78:5–7

THE ONLY WAY to live a life of complete obedience to God is to know His commandments. As I mentioned previously, the Hebrew word translated "law" in Psalm 78:5 is *torah*, a word that refers to the first five books of the Bible—inspired writings that contain the Mosaic Law. According to Jewish tradition, the Torah contains 613 commandments (365 negative commandments and 248 affirmative ones). Not all of these are required of God's people now because of Jesus's coming and the fact that He fulfilled the law. However, we are not without law. The Bible says we are "under the law toward Christ" (1 Cor. 9:21). In other words, obedience to the currently applicable commandments should result from our devotion to the Lord Jesus.

You would think that with the establishment of the new covenant— the covenant that celebrates the grace of God—the number of commandments would decrease. Actually, the opposite has happened. There are approximately 1,050 in the New Testament; however, the emphasis is no longer on just keeping rigid rules and regulations. Jesus shifted our attention upward to the "first great commandment" (loving God with all our heart, mind, soul, and strength), and the second that is "like it" (loving our neighbor as ourselves). The Messiah insisted, "On these two commandments hang all the Law and the Prophets" (Matt. 22:40). If we teach our children this dual-emphasis in life—loving God and loving others—all other commandments should fall into place.

Prayer Declaration

*Lord God Almighty, I declare that we as a family are account-
able to You. I submit to Your authority and believe in Your commandments. I trust in Your promise to write Your law within my
heart—and I pray You will do the same for my child, that we may
have a natural, inborn inclination to walk in Your ways. I pray
that _____ will willingly embrace the first great commandment to love God with all his/her heart, and the second great
commandment, which is to love others as we love ourselves. As
these complementary attitudes take over my child's heart and life,
keeping the rest of Your commandments will automatically ensue.
I pass this knowledge to my child, believing _____ will
have a passion to live within Your revealed will for humankind. In
the name of Jesus, amen (let it be so)!*

MATURE PLANTS

Rescue me and deliver me from the hand of foreigners, whose
mouth speaks lying words, and whose right hand is a right hand of
falsehood—that our sons may be as plants grown up in their youth;
that our daughters may be as pillars, sculptured in palace style.
—PSALM 144:11–12

THIS IS A parent's prayerful plea to be delivered from the deceitful influence of the ungodly so that he can be a good role model for his offspring. Children normally imitate their parents. If we succeed in bearing fruit for the kingdom, our children are more likely to do the same. Both sons and daughters become as "plants grown up in their youth"—in other words, having been "planted" in the truth at an early age, they tend to mature spiritually at a more rapid pace.

Timothy was a pastor in the early church and, apparently, was quite young. We assume this because Paul told him, "Let no one despise your youth" (1 Tim. 4:12). He must have developed in God quickly because "from childhood" he knew "the Holy Scriptures" (2 Tim. 3:15). Genuine faith was evidenced in him, for it first resided in his grandmother Lois, then his mother, Eunice. A wonderful legacy was passed to him.

I have witnessed this many times in ministry-minded families. There is no greater modern-day example than Pastor Tommy Barnett, a friend I greatly admire who started preaching in his teens. He watched his own father minister to the poor and downtrodden for years. He admits, "Some things are taught; some are caught. I really caught my 'giving-ness' from my dad."[1]

Now Pastor Tommy has passed the torch to his children, who have grown into "mature plants." Matthew Barnett pastors the Dream Center in Los Angeles, an incredible church that has become a model worldwide for 24/7 ministry, especially to the poor and the oppressed. May your child also catch your passion for God and become a mature plant at an early age.

Prayer Declaration

Lord God, help me to walk in genuine faith, then reproduce the same in my son/daughter. I have "planted" _____ "in the house of the Lord" (Ps. 92:13). Therefore, as Scripture promises, I expect him/her to flourish in the things of God. Awaken in my child the understanding that earthly things are temporary and heavenly things are eternal—and give him/her a desire for those things that endure forever. I confess that _____ will mature in God at an early age. Even as Hannah "planted" her son Samuel in God's house and he became a "mature plant" early in life—receiving supernatural visitations as a young boy (1 Sam. 1–3)—so let it be for my child. In the name of Jesus, amen (let it be so)!

PILLARS OF TRUTH

That our sons may be as plants grown up in their youth; that our daughters may be as pillars, sculptured in palace style.
—PSALM 144:12

PILLARS OFTEN SYMBOLIZE inspiring traits such as strength, wisdom, uprightness, authority, and resolve—characteristics that make good leaders. It takes believers who will stand like pillars to uphold God's work in this world; flimsy spiritual props will just give way under the pressure.

When Jeremiah was but a child, God said He would make him like "an iron pillar"—immovable in the face of opposition (Jer. 1:18). The church as a whole is described as a "pillar...of the truth" (1 Tim. 3:15). So every member of the church—adult or child—should exhibit "pillar-like" qualities and fill the role of world changers and history makers. All overcoming believers have the eternal destiny of being "pillars in the temple of God"—which is certainly a prophetic description of our role in the government of God to come (Rev. 3:12). Since we have claimed our children to partake of this exalted status, we can expect them to be "sculptured in palace style" at an early age—developed as the supportive columns of a divine purpose that stretches from time to eternity.

PRAYER DECLARATION

Lord God, thank You for making my child like a pillar— unmovable, and unchanging in his/her commitment to You. Let my child be wise, upright, full of authority, determined, and excellent in all things. I pray _____ will be like Jeremiah and will stand for the truth (like an iron pillar) even when it is unpopular. Finally, I confess by faith that _____ will ultimately be like a pillar "sculptured in palace style," an eternal pillar in the temple of God, one who will rule with God over all things in the kingdom that is to come. In the name of Jesus, amen (let it be so)!

POLISHED CORNERSTONES

Rid me, and deliver me from the hand of strange children, whose mouth speaketh vanity, and their right hand is a right hand of falsehood: that our sons may be as plants grown up in their youth; that our daughters may be as corner stones, polished after the similitude of a palace.
—PSALM 144:11–12, KJV

THE KING JAMES Version of Psalm 144:12 describes the daughters of God's people as cornerstones, not pillars. A cornerstone is the beginning of a structure to which the rest of the building conforms in style, size, slant, and shape. I believe this symbol speaks especially of those who are used of God to initiate His unique purposes in the earth.

The most dominant example is the Lord Jesus Himself, referred to as the "chief cornerstone" in Ephesians 2:20. He was the initial stone of a spiritual building that God began erecting in the earth nearly two thousand years ago in order to inhabit it with His glory. The "construction" of this living cathedral, spanning two millennia, was definitely a new approach, a new revelation—something the Bible calls a "new covenant" (Jer. 31:31).

If Jesus was the chief cornerstone—and His sons and daughters bear His image—believers should *all* fill the role of lesser cornerstones. We are called to be initiators, innovators, visionaries, history makers, and world changers—purpose-driven people used of God to start new trends so His divine designs can be fulfilled. It is not presumptuous or preposterous for me to say these things, because we are all "His workmanship, created in Christ Jesus for good works, which God prepared beforehand that we should walk in them" (Eph. 2:10). We all have a purpose. We can all begin something of great value, even if on a small scale.

Prayer Declaration

Lord God, I pray that You will give my child the courage to be an individual, to stand for what is right, and to be creative in serving You day by day. I confess that You will initiate something of great value through _____ that the world might be a better place. Empower him/her to be a cornerstone, a trendsetter, establishing divinely inspired plans and purposes in the earth. Give me grace to prepare my child, not for the "shack" of mediocrity but for the "palace" of excellence, polishing _____ so his/her gifts and callings are fully manifested. In the name of Jesus, amen (let it be so)!

A GOOD LIFE

*I will give them singleness of heart and singleness of pur-
pose, so that they will fear me forever—this will be for their
own good and for the good of their children after them.*
—JEREMIAH 32:39, CJB

NEVER COMPROMISING, NEVER accepting defeat, never wavering
from God's perfect will—adopting such high standards is a good
sign that God has given us "singleness of heart." If we as parents sin-
cerely attempt to live this way—pleasing God alone—Jeremiah foretells
two good things that will happen. First, it will result in a good life for
us—a life that is full of purpose, full of peace, and full of fruit. Second,
our lifestyle becomes a pattern for our children to follow. Living out the
good life before them—and reaping its benefits—should awaken in them
the desire to follow in our footsteps.

Of course, you might be whispering, "Reality check—that all sounds
real nice, but as much as I try, I haven't been consistent. I haven't stayed
focused." It is never too late to start over. God loves to forget the past
and grant new beginnings. It helps to see that this promise was originally given to a generation that miserably failed God. Defeated by the
Babylonians, they lost everything and were forced into slavery. But God
promised they would be restored to their homeland. If they could pick
up the pieces and start again, so can you.

Then again, you may have been consistent in living the good life, but
it appears your child is bent toward serving the world. First of all, don't
blame yourself. Second, don't give up—keep claiming this promise. God
is a good God. He sends good and perfect gifts from above (James 1:17).
Let's believe He will perform a "good work" (Phil. 1:6) in your child
supernaturally, and you and your child will both "flow together to the
goodness of the LORD" (Jer. 31:12, KJV).

Prayer Declaration

Lord God, first I repent of any inconsistencies that have been in my life. Forgive me for those times I've failed as a parent to model a Christlike walk before my child. I pray You will grant me singleness of heart and singleness of purpose that I may never depart from the things of God. I pray this unwavering determination will also be awakened in _____ so that both of us can truly experience a good life to the highest possible degree, filled and overflowing with the goodness of the Lord. In the name of Jesus, amen (let it be so)!

EXPERIENCING THE GLORY OF GOD

Let Your work appear to Your servants, and Your glory to their children.
—PSALM 90:16

MOSES WROTE PSALM 90 under the influence of the Holy Spirit. We know this because "all Scripture is given by inspiration of God" (2 Tim. 3:16). The word *inspiration* used in that passage means to breathe into. Psalm 90 was much more than just a prophet interceding for the nation of Israel. It was the Holy Spirit "breathing into" that prophet a petition that concerned all of God's people in every era.

Whenever the Holy Spirit prays, the Father answers—without a doubt. So according to this prayer, if we are servants of God, we can expect to see God work in our lives and manifest His glory to our children.

The glory of the Lord is primarily His manifested presence (as was seen on Mount Sinai, in Solomon's temple, and in the Upper Room). The glory of God also refers to demonstrations of His power that bring honor and praise to His name. The Holy Spirit has already interceded for our children through Moses. It is our responsibility to believe, confess, and praise God for the fulfillment of His divine design.

PRAYER DECLARATION

Lord God, I declare that I am a servant of God. I renew my commitment to serve Your purposes in this world. Because I am yielded in this way, I expect You to work in my life, and I expect to participate in Your works in this world. I also confess by faith in this promise that Your glory will be manifested to my child. I praise You for supernaturally revealing Your power and greatness to _____ that praise might flow from his/her life upward to Your throne. Lord, I trust You to do glorious things—in, for, and through my child—that will bring glory to Your name forevermore. In the name of Jesus, amen (let it be so)!

AN INHERITANCE FROM THE LORD

Children are an inheritance from the LORD. They are a reward from him.
—PSALM 127:3, GW

THOSE WHO LEAVE an inheritance for their heirs transfer their legacy in several ways. They leave a heritage of what they have, what they do, and a greater legacy (for those who are Christlike) of who they are. According to our key verse, children are part of the inheritance God gives His people. God is the Creator—that's who He is—and one of His most wonderful abilities is the capacity to create—that's what He does. So as part of our inheritance God has passed on to us procreative ability, which I believe is one of the greatest gifts we could have.

It is a profound thing that a man and woman can unite in marriage and impart their image and likeness to their offspring. Furthermore, when any child is conceived, he or she contains a soul that will live forever! God could have reserved this creative ability for Himself, but He rejoiced to share with us a powerful reflection of who He is and what He does.

PRAYER DECLARATION

Lord God, first I thank You for my child. I receive _____ as an inheritance from You. I praise You that my image and values are being passed to my son/daughter. I am a co-laborer with You, creatively working—both naturally and spiritually—to fill the earth with God-loving people. I thank You for the ability to transfer to my child an inheritance of what I have, but more importantly, an inheritance of who I am and what I do. I am a servant of God, a child of God, and a member of the bride of Christ, married to You forever. These glorious facets of my identity I bequeath to _____ by faith. May he/she receive this inheritance with gratitude and faith, and then become "an inheritance from the Lord" that is passed to the next generation. In the name of Jesus, amen (let it be so)!

GOD'S REWARD

Children are an inheritance from the LORD. They are a reward from him.
—PSALM 127:3, GW

A REWARD IS SOMETHING given in return for good behavior or exceptional performance. According to Hebrews 11:6, those who come to God must first "believe that He is, and that He is a rewarder of those who diligently seek Him." This is the nature of God. He so enjoys compensating His offspring for their service that when the Lord returns, "His reward" will be "with Him" (Isa. 62:11). Yet rewards are reserved not only for the future; God rewards us in this life as well.

In our key passage God declares the "fruit of the womb is his reward" (KJV). So one of the ways God blesses us is by sending children into our lives. Children are meant to bring joy, fulfillment, and the perpetuation of our name and values. Unfortunately, for some believers the opposite happens. For a season their children bring sorrow and heartbreak; they discard their parents' values and even reject their faith. Should parents in this situation succumb to depression and just give up? *No way!* Instead they need to reaffirm over and over—as we all should—that our children are truly a reward from God. Confessing this truth in faith has the power to turn any situation around.

PRAYER DECLARATION

Lord God, I claim this passage by faith: that my child is part of the inheritance You have given Me. _____ is a gift from God, a reward from You. I confess and believe that he/she will fulfill the role You intended and will perpetuate biblical values in the earth. I have planted many seeds of truth in _____. I believe that he/she will bear much fruit for the kingdom and ultimately receive a great reward from God as well. In the name of Jesus, amen (let it be so)!

A REAL BLESSING

Children are a gift from the Lord; they are a real blessing.
—Psalm 127:3, GNT

WHEN GOD FIRST appeared to Abraham, He promised, "I will bless you…and you shall be a blessing…and in you all the families of the earth shall be blessed" (Gen. 12:2–3). Later on He pledged, "In your seed all the nations of the earth shall be blessed" (Gen. 22:18). God promised to bless Abraham by giving him children; then God promised to use those children to bless all the families of the earth—of every nation, race, and culture. What a blessing it is to have children who bear your image, both naturally and spiritually! What a blessing to have them return your love! What a blessing to see them mature and fulfill their dreams! But what an even greater blessing it is to see them bless others with the truth and expand God's blessing around the globe! This is what it means to be a real blessing, and this is what I claim for you and yours!

PRAYER DECLARATION

Lord God, I know Galatians 3:9 announces that those who are "of faith" are "blessed with faithful Abraham" (KJV). I declare that one of my greatest blessings will be the continuation of God's blessing through my offspring. I confess that _____ is, and will be, a great blessing to me. But more importantly, my child will be a blessing to You and to many others while in this world. May this blessing of God flow so powerfully through _____ that it ultimately extends around the globe in its influence. In the name of Jesus, amen (let it be so)!

SPIRITUAL WEAPONS

*Behold, children are a heritage from the LORD, the fruit of the womb
is a reward. Like arrows in the hand of a warrior, so are the children
of one's youth. Happy is the man who has his quiver full of them. They
shall not be ashamed, but shall speak with their enemies in the gate.*
—PSALM 127:3–5

ARROWS IN THE hand of a warrior"—what a peculiar way of describing the children of God-loving parents! Yet when we consider the global spiritual war raging over the souls of all human beings, it makes sense that godly parents would be likened to "warriors." Good parents daily fight the good fight of faith against spiritual darkness in their own lives and the lives of others.

Prayerful mothers and fathers often receive inspired insights concerning their children's gifts. The God-given responsibility of these parents is to "load" their sons and daughters in the "bow" of a life pulled "tight" with commitment and then "shoot" them toward their divine destiny.

The more children you have serving God and fulfilling His purpose, the greater your happiness. The Contemporary English Version translates Psalm 127:5 this way: "The more you have, the better off you will be, because they will protect you when your enemies attack." When you teach your children how to be "weapons for righteousness" in God's hands, they will be equipped to come to your rescue in time of need (Rom. 6:13, HCSB).

PRAYER DECLARATION

*Lord God of hosts, You are a God of war. You are currently fighting
evil principalities and powers for the control of this world. I declare
that my child is not only an arrow in my quiver, but according to
Isaiah 49:2, he/she is an arrow in Your quiver as well—a weapon*

in the hands of the almighty God. Give me grace to know the target of my child's destiny, so that as Your hand extended I can shoot _____ toward the bull's-eye of the perfect will of God for his/her life. I pray that _____ will be used of God to win great spiritual battles, so that the kingdom of God might advance in this world. Whenever the enemy tries to slip through an entrance ("a gate") into our family circle, let me be unashamed as a parent as I watch _____ oppose all satanic plots, defending "the gate" and conquering valiantly for the cause of Christ. In the name of Jesus, amen (let it be so)!

CHOSEN BY GOD

*Out of heaven He let you hear His voice, that He might instruct
you; on earth He showed you His great fire, and you heard His
words out of the midst of the fire. And because He loved your fathers,
therefore He chose their descendants after them; and He brought
you out of Egypt with His Presence, with His mighty power.*
—DEUTERONOMY 4:36–37

A CCORDING TO THIS passage, one of God's primary motivations
for choosing to favor the nation of Israel was simply His love for
their forefathers Abraham, Isaac, and Jacob. In Deuteronomy 7:7–8, He
added that He chose Israel because of the "oath which He swore" to
the patriarchs—not because the Israelites were a great nation. Quite the
contrary, they were the "least of all peoples."

God's personality has not changed. True Christians are deeply loved
of God, just as the patriarchs were. Therefore it is believable that He will
treat their offspring in a similar way, acknowledging them as His "special treasure" (v. 6). Of course, in the new covenant God has opened His
heart and His arms to the entire human race and not just one particular
nation or people group. However, the offspring of the righteous are still
very important to Him.

PRAYER DECLARATION

*Lord God, I love You with all of my heart. I am convinced that
You also love me with an everlasting love, and nothing can separate
me from Your love. You have surrounded my family with wonderful promises. Because of the bond of love between You and me, I
believe You will choose my child as Your special treasure—leading,
instructing, blessing, and helping _____ in numerous
ways that he/she might fulfill Your purposes for time and eternity.
In the name of Jesus, amen (let it be so)!*

EVERLASTING LIFE

"For as the new heavens and the new earth which I will
make shall remain before Me," says the LORD, *"so shall*
your descendants and your name remain."
—ISAIAH 66:22

THERE IS NO greater pledge from the lips of God than this: that our offspring will abide in His presence forever. According to this verse, such an expectation is just as stable and unchanging as the new creation. God longs for a restored universe free from evil, permeated with peace, and immersed in His infinite love. More than that, He longs for the day when both we and our descendants are transformed fully into His image—perfected, glorified, and shining like the sun in the kingdom of our Father.

Does this mean that our children will live eternally in a flawless, heavenly state, whether they personally choose to serve God or not? Certainly not! However, it does mean that the Father will honor our commitment to Him by extending extraordinary grace to our children in enabling them to make the right choices. He will go beyond the norm in helping them to follow the path that leads to an infinite inheritance.

When God was preparing to judge Sodom and Gomorrah, the Bible says God "remembered" Abraham and "saved Lot from the terrible destruction" (Gen. 19:29, CEV). Although Lot was just Abraham's nephew, he and his family escaped the torrent of fiery brimstone that fell just because of their connection to Abraham. How much more will God do this kind of thing for the children of His people! We must believe this enough to thank God in advance, claiming 1 John 2:25 for the whole family: "This is the promise that He has promised *us*—eternal life" (emphasis added).

Prayer Declaration

Lord God, I believe my child's eternal destiny is secure with You. In all of his/her struggles in life, I believe You will remember my commitment to You and save _____ from this destructive world. You are the Almighty, and the intentions of Your heart will be fulfilled. You intend to bring forth a new creation (a new heaven and a new earth): free from darkness, free from pain, free from evil, free from satanic influence, and free from the curse. Nothing will change this divine purpose or prevent it from coming to pass. In like manner I believe that You intend to make my child a new creation, granting him/her the grace to love You, to serve You, and to abide in Your presence forever (2 Cor. 5:17). I confess that _____ will also be free from darkness, free from pain, free from evil, free from satanic influence, and free from the curse forever. As the new creation shall remain before You—filled with Your presence and made perfect in every way—so shall my offspring remain: perfected in God forevermore. In the name of Jesus, amen (let it be so)!

REVELATION

The secret things belong to the LORD our God, but those things which are revealed belong to us and to our children forever, that we may do all the words of this law.
—DEUTERONOMY 29:29

THERE ARE SOME mysteries, or "secret things," concerning God, the universe, and humanity that we may never fully comprehend in this life. But there are revealed truths that we can count among our most precious possessions. When God reveals truth, it changes us permanently so that we can change the world around us with the same truth. There are many biblical examples of key revelations that brought about great personal, national, and even global transformations.

- God revealed Himself to Noah, and the human race was saved from extinction (Gen. 6–9).

- God revealed Himself to Abraham, and a covenant nation was born (Gen. 17).

- God revealed Himself to Moses, and Israel was delivered from slavery (Exod. 3–12).

- God revealed Himself to Saul (later to be named Paul), and the door to the Gentiles swung open wide (Acts 9).

Now God has revealed Himself to you in a very special way. He has opened your understanding concerning the sixty-five promises bestowed on the children of the righteous. This revelation belongs to *you* and to *your child*, and nothing can steal it from you. Go ahead—expect results just as dramatic on a personal level as the building of the ark, the miracle birth of Isaac, the collapse of the Egyptian empire, and the gospel spreading to every nation. If revealed truth could accomplish such great feats of faith for others, just what will it accomplish for you and your child? Start praising God now for the miracle that you need.

Prayer Declaration

Lord God, I thank You for all the revelations You have given me, especially this revelation of the promises You have bestowed on the children of Your people. This insight belongs to me. I claim it as a gift from God. It belongs to my child, _____, also. Nothing can steal it from us. It is part of the wonderful inheritance You have imparted to us. This awesome truth has come into our home—to bless, to change, and to transform us that we might bring blessing, change, and transformation to the world. I pray and believe that You will activate these promises on our behalf, Lord, but more than that, I believe You will use us to activate these promises in the lives of others. I declare that this blessing will not end with us; it will keep passing from one life to another until it encircles the globe. In the name of Jesus, amen (let it be so)!

More things are wrought by prayer than this world dreams of.
Wherefore, let thy voice rise like a fountain for me night and day.[1]
—Alfred Lord Tennyson

There is always a moment in childhood when
the door opens and lets the future in.[2]
—Graham Greene

CONCLUSION

YOUR FAITH WILL MAKE
THE DIFFERENCE

*Children rarely experience breakthroughs on their own. Left
alone, few will travel quickly down the road to their potential. They need their parents to help them along.*[3]
—JOHN C. MAXWELL

HEBREWS 11:1 REMINDS us that "faith is the substance of things
hoped for, the evidence of things not seen." By now your faith
should be soaring. What you've just read really is true. God gave these
promises, and He intends to keep them.

Jacob made a coat of many colors for his favored son, Joseph, and
placed it upon him as a sign of his great love. In a similar way, by
claiming and confessing these sixty-five God-given promises you have
woven a spiritual rainbow-colored garment and lovingly placed it upon
your child. What a powerful thing you have done! What a pivotal point
in your relationship! What an impartation of favor toward them—from
God and from you!

The original coat of many colors was symbolic of Joseph's calling from
God—His anointing, that invisible covering from the heavenly Father
that propelled him mightily and successfully through all the challenging
circumstances he faced in life. First he was rejected and betrayed, then
enslaved, then falsely accused and imprisoned in Pharaoh's dungeon.
Against all odds the spiritual garment Joseph wore—the anointing on
his life—took him from the bottom to the top in one day when Pharaoh
appointed him prime minister over all of Egypt.

Let it be so for your offspring as well! May these promises be a garment of favor that propels your child through every life challenge and
into the glorious destiny and divine purpose that awaits.

A Rainbow of Promise

It has already been sufficiently proven that God's blessing passes down the family line from consecrated foreparents, for "He remembers His covenant forever, the Word which He commanded, for *a thousand generations*" (Ps. 105:8, emphasis added). The length of a generation is not exactly defined in Scripture. It could be anywhere from twenty to one hundred years (though it seems from Psalm 95:10 that it is most likely forty years). But no matter what figure you use to represent a generation, you have a huge stretch of time if you multiply it by a thousand— somewhere between twenty thousand to one hundred thousand years.

How powerful it is that your walk with God could have such a lingering influence! And if the overflow of your relationship with God can persist that far into the future—long after you are gone and your name forgotten—how much more will it bring God's power and blessing upon those generations immediately following you! This is a powerful truth, but it gets even better.

Let's examine God's pledge to Noah. After this great patriarch and his family were kept safe for about a year in the ark, the floodwaters subsided. Then God brought them out to see an awesome sight: the first spectacular, color-filled rainbow stretching across the sky. The Most High explained to Noah the reason behind such an impressive display of divine artistry.

> And God said: "This is the sign of the covenant which I make between Me and you, and every living creature that is with you, for perpetual generations: I set My rainbow in the cloud, and it shall be for the sign of the covenant between Me and the earth. It shall be, when I bring a cloud over the earth, that the rainbow shall be seen in the cloud; and I will remember My covenant which is between Me and you and every living creature of all flesh; the waters shall never again become a flood to destroy all flesh.
>
> —Genesis 9:12–15

Not only was this a covenant promise to Noah, but it also was a covenant promise to all his seed—for perpetual generations. Here we are, millennia later, the righteous and the wicked, still benefiting from this covenant commitment, and we can trust that it will be kept. The earth will never be submerged again. Period.

Why not expect something just as powerful and long lasting in God's commitment to you? Noah's God is your God. His nature is the same. His ways have not changed. He may even give you a sign too (especially if you ask Him) of His dedication to your family. (Asking for a "sign" is biblically acceptable; see Isaiah 7:11.)

Know that your relationship with God has positioned all of your offspring under a spiritual kind of rainbow, an arc of hope, a multicolored band of sixty-five divine pledges. These promises will remain over them, "living and powerful" (Heb. 4:12) "for perpetual generations" (Gen. 9:12), stretching into the future with never-ending influence, which is an even greater and more lasting pledge than the "thousand generations" commitment of Psalm 105:8.

So quit allowing fear to cloud your view. Stop being apprehensive and worried, picturing your offspring as weak, vulnerable, impressionable, beset by the world and wearing the rags of carnality, or buffeted by the storms of life. Instead *see* your seed standing strong, confident, unafraid, and blessed of God—each one wearing a coat of many colors (the sign of God's favor, a treasured family heirloom that can be traced back to you) and abiding under a "rainbow of promise" (a covenant sign of God's power to bring you and your offspring out of every storm).

Oh, and remember one more thing—WYSIWYG! What does that mean? It's an acronym—one I hope you will never forget: *What You Say Is What You Get.*

So don't just *see* this condition for your seed—*say it,* as often as you can. Declare, "My child is clothed in a spiritual coat of many colors!" and, "My child abides under a rainbow of promise that stretches from the beginning to the end of his/her life!" The more you say it, the more you will believe it. The more you believe it, the more likely you are to see God create optimum spiritual conditions in your child's life.

I urged you to embrace the power of confession in the beginning of this book. I cannot overemphasize it now that we are coming to the end. But let me underscore an important, additional piece of essential information: don't put your faith in some repetitious confession; put your faith in *the great and mighty God* who watches over His Word (as you confess it) to perform it on your behalf. And then abide in *hope*—which, by the way, is a power word that provides another great acronym: *Having Only Positive Expectations.*

Two Powerful Symbols

Have you ever noticed the small black boxes Jewish men wear on their foreheads and upper arms, especially during prayer? These objects are called "frontlets" in the Old Testament and "phylacteries" in the New (Exod. 13:16; Matt. 23:5). If you were to open one of these boxes, which traditionally also are called "tefillin," you would find either four strips of parchment in four chambers (the head tefillin) or one four-columned strip of parchment in one chamber (the arm tefillin).

On the parchment are four hand-written passages of Scripture: Exodus 13:1–10, Exodus 13:11–16, Deuteronomy 6:4–9, and Deuteronomy 11:13–21. These passages reveal essential truths for God's people still today, but they were part of the law for the Israelites of old. You should read these references when you can, just to get a better understanding of this custom.

A related tradition is the mounting of something called a "mezuzah" on the gates and doorposts of Jewish homes. The mezuzah is a hand-written parchment housed in a small rectangular box, normally about four to eight inches in length and about one to two inches in width. This ornamental container, which may be made of wood, metal, glass, or ceramic, contains two of the four Bible passages found in the phylacteries: Deuteronomy 6:4–9 and Deuteronomy 11:13–21. When observant Jewish families enter their homes, they will normally touch or kiss the mezuzah as a worshipful sign. Every time they do this, they are reaffirming the promises contained within that box and their belief that the

God of Abraham is protecting their home, watching over their family, and executing these promises in their behalf.

Four verses in one of the key passages in the mezuzah explain the purpose of these two related customs (the wearing of tefillin and the mounting of mezuzahs). The Most High, the King of the universe, commands:

> Therefore you shall lay up these words of mine in your heart and in your soul, and bind them as *a sign on your hand*, and they shall be *as frontlets between your eyes*. You shall teach them to your children, speaking of them when you sit in your house, when you walk by the way, when you lie down, and when you rise up. And you shall write them on the doorposts of your house and on your gates [the mezuzah], that your days and the days of your children may be multiplied in the land of which the LORD swore to your fathers to give them, like the days of the heavens above the earth.
> —DEUTERONOMY 11:18–21, EMPHASIS ADDED

If you are Jewish, you likely already understand the spiritual implications of these customs. If you are not Jewish, you may be wondering how to relate this information to your life. Take it figuratively and relate it to the insight contained within this book. You will probably never wear a frontlet on your forehead, but these sixty-five promises can dominate your thinking until you are more convinced of these divine pledges than any negative circumstance you are facing with your child. Also, you will probably never literally wear a tefillin on your arm, but you can let the sixty-five promises in this book guide the relationship you have with your offspring. That's what the arm and hand symbolize—how you interact with others and the love you express.

Concerning these two traditions (tefillin and mezuzahs), pastor Ed Young points out that the "Deuteronomy passage lays out the principle of establishing an environment full of God's Word and truth. A family is to be saturated with the understanding of His principles for living."[4] To put these practices into a new covenant perspective, you might consider doing the following:

+ Write some of the promises you have studied on index cards and post them around your home, on your refrigerator, or at the entrance to your child's room as a constant, daily reminder.

+ Touch and confess these posted promises from time to time in a worshipful gesture toward God, praising Him for their fulfillment.

+ Speak to your child about these promises. Without being overbearing, weave them into your conversations in creative ways as often as you can.

Do this "that your days and the days of your children may be multiplied...like the days of the heavens above the earth" (Deut. 11:21).

Phylacteries are small leather boxes with long straps that allow worshippers to wear the boxes on their foreheads and on their arms. Inside the boxes are four passages from the Torah (Exod. 13:1–10; 13:11–16; Deut. 6:4–9; 11:13–21). A phylactery worn on the left arm is a reminder to keep God's law with all your heart. The one worn on the forehead is to remind the wearer to focus his concentration on the law.

A mezuzah is a sacred parchment inscribed with passages from the Torah. Observant Jewish families place it in a protective case and hang it on the doorposts of their homes. The case itself is also referred to as a mezuzah.

UNDER THE SHADOW OF THE ALMIGHTY

Always remember: you are under God's authority—and your child is under your authority—so there is an overflow of divine influence that passes through you into your offspring's life. You have clout in heaven; you have friends in high places. The Most High God honors your position as a parent. Much as Boaz did for Ruth when she lay at the wealthy landowner's feet (Ruth 3), God casts His garment of spiritual authority over you. It is a redemptive cloak of protection, provision, and power, and that covering affects both you and your offspring.

One of my favorite Bible verses is Psalm 91:1: "He who dwells in the secret place of the Most High shall abide under the shadow of the Almighty." First, I want you to notice the two primary parts of this sentence. The first phrase presents God's mandate—that believers dwell in His secret place (a place of communion and commitment). The second phrase presents His promised response—that He will overshadow us all the days of our lives.

Consider also the two names of God revealed in this verse: *El-Elyon*, translated "Most High," and *El-Shaddai*, which means "Almighty." This divine commitment is made to individuals who dwell in "the secret place of the *Most High*." In other words, it is for those who acknowledge God as the Most High in their lives—higher than anything or anyone else. These devoted persons are then privileged to "abide under the shadow of the *Almighty*," under the covering of God's all-sufficient protection, provision, and power.

Your offspring come under the same overshadowing promise by default. Because of your walk with God, this invisible spiritual canopy spreads over their earthly existence, with very visible results.

One of my most vivid childhood memories illustrates this truth wonderfully. Back in the late 1950s my mother and all four of us children were flying back to Guantanamo Bay, Cuba, where my father was stationed. Unknown to us, right when the plane landed in Santiago, Castro and his forces were descending upon the city to seize it. The airport was shut down, so we were not able to catch our flight.

That night was a very scary experience for me as a six-year-old. My mother, brother, two sisters, and me were escorted to a motel room (a dingy and dirty room, but a great comfort nonetheless), but there was no sleeping. Guns were cracking and bullets flying as the rebels streamed through the alleys and streets. All of us huddled together on the grimy floor. Mom explained that if we would lay down on the ground, any bullets passing through the walls or window of the room would be less likely to hit us.

When my father found out about our dilemma, he quickly obtained an official car from the naval base. The car had an American flag flying from the antenna and was often used to escort important officials. Dad dressed in his full military regalia, with all his medals and stripes as a commander in the US Navy, and drove over treacherous mountain roads to find his family. He made it past all the roadblocks and stakeouts because when they saw the car and my father's uniform, the insurgents waved him on with no problem.

Once we were in the car, Dad told all of us children to crouch down on the floorboard between the front and back seats. To this day I remember looking up in awe at the stream of soldiers marching by with rifles held to their shoulders. Most of them kept their eyes straight ahead, as if they were oblivious to us. I didn't fully understand what was happening; I just knew that once my father got there, we were safe.

When the rebel soldiers stared at the car, their gaze tended to shift toward the red, white, and blue flag that identified our citizenship. They must have assumed that the adults riding inside were untouchable, high-ranking military personnel. Because my father was submitted to the authority of the chain of command above him, there was a transfer of authority down to him—from the president of the United States and his cabinet to the Congress and the Senate to the Pentagon and the joint chiefs of staff, all the way down to this one naval commander, Andrew Shreve, passing through enemy territory.

There were no other high-ranking government or military officers riding with him, but my father was surrounded by an invisible host—the multiplied thousands of men and women serving in the US military. The guerrillas knew if they harmed or injured us in any way, they might be inviting a united response from the US government—something they were not prepared to face at that point. So because my father was under the "shadow" of the US government, he was safe—and because we were under our father's "shadow," we were safe.

So it is for you and your children. Your offspring may be behind enemy lines. Go after them, just as my father did. Put on your "military garments"—the whole armor of God (Eph. 6:10–12). Wave the bloodstained banner of Calvary as you claim your children in prayer—and bring them back home. You are not alone. The Lord of hosts, the commander of an army of angels, has sent forth His ministering spirits to watch over you and your offspring. You are under God's shadow, and they are under yours.

Believe this with all your heart. Believe this with all your mind. Believe this with all your might. Your faith will make the difference. A miracle is already in motion for you and your family. Let it come to pass—for the glory of God and the praise of His name!

PRAISE AND PROGRESS JOURNAL

THE FOLLOWING SECTION is designed to help you keep a written account of how God leads you to pray for your child and the ways He answers those prayers. If you need more space to write or if you are reading this book electronically, consider purchasing a separate journal to record scriptures God gives you to declare over your child, impressions you receive from the Holy Spirit, and the many praise reports you will witness through the years. If you have more than one child, I recommend that you keep a separate journal or copy of this book for each offspring.

Family Vision Statement

The Bible says, "Where there is no vision, the people perish" (Prov. 29:18, KJV). Write a vision and mission statement for your family, and share it with your offspring. Let it guide you and your children in fulfilling God's plan for your lives. I suggest you make it a declaration concerning the gifts and potential abilities that reside within your child—and a declaration concerning the fruit that you believe will result when these gifts are fully awakened and manifested. It would probably be good for you to create two parts to the vision statement: your vision for your child (or each individual child if you have two or more) and your vision for what the family as a whole should and could accomplish both naturally and spiritually. You could also break it up into segments of five, ten, or twenty years.

Praise Reports

Psalm 103:2 tells us to "praise the Lord...and never forget all the good he has done" (GW). Use the space below to record the ways God answered your prayers and brought breakthrough in your family. Keep this as a reminder of His goodness and faithfulness to you and your children.

Personal Prayers

The prayers included in this book are meant to guide you through declaring the sixty-five promises. But as God gives you even more specific ways to pray for your children, write them down here. Then when God responds to your petition, remember to record the victory with your praise reports.

PERSONAL CONFESSIONS

As God gives you scriptures addressing a unique situation you or your children may be facing, record them here and declare God's Word over that circumstance. Confess the Word until there is a breakthrough.

Memorable Happenings

Use this book to record milestones in your child's life and memorable moments for your family. Even when he or she is an adult, your child will cherish these memories.

NOTES

INTRODUCTION
A MIRACLE FOR YOUR FAMILY

1. *Merriam-Webster's Collegiate Dictionary*, 11th edition (Springfield, MA: Merriam-Webster, Inc., 2003), s.v. "miracle."
2. Jack Hayford, ed., *Spirit-Filled Life Bible* (Nashville: Thomas Nelson Publishers, 1991), 6.
3. ThinkExist.com, "Zig Ziglar Quotes, http://thinkexist .com/quotation/when_you_put_faith-hope_and_love_ together-you_can/145457.html (accessed October 5, 2012).
4. E. M. Bounds, *E.M. Bounds: The Classic Collection on Prayer*, Harold J. Chadwick, ed. (Alachua, FL: Bridge-Logos Publishers, 2001), 199.
5. Diana Loomans, "If I Had My Child to Raise Over Again," in *100 Ways to Build Self-Esteem and Teach Values* (Novato, CA: New World Library, 1994, 2003), 213. www .dianaloomans.com. Used by permission.
6. *Merriam-Webster's Collegiate Dictionary*, s.v. "promise."

43
WEALTH

1. As quoted in William J. Federer, *America's God and Country: Encyclopedia of Quotations* (St. Louis, MO: Amerisearch, Inc., 1994), 433.

51
HOPE IN GOD

1. As quoted in John Maxwell, *Think on These Things: Meditations for Leaders* (Kansas City, MO: Beacon Hill Press, 1999), 149.

54
Mature Plants

1. Tommy Barnett, *Hidden Power* (Lake Mary, FL: Charisma House, 2002), 40–41.

Conclusion
Your Faith Will Make the Difference

1. Alfred Lord Tennyson, "Morte D'Arthur," http://library.sc.edu/spcoll/britlit/tenn/morte.html (accessed October 9, 2012).
2. Graham Greene, *The Power and the Glory* (New York: Penguin, 1990), 12.
3. John C. Maxwell, *Breakthrough Parenting* (Colorado Springs, CO: Focus on the Family Publications, 1996), 6.
4. Ed Young, *The 10 Commandments of Parenting* (Chicago: Moody Publishers, 2005), 158.

FOR FURTHER INFORMATION, CONTACT:

Mike Shreve
P. O. Box 4260
Cleveland, TN 37320
www.shreveministries.org
mikeshreve@shreveministries.org
Phone: 423-478-2843